IN THIS TIME of MERCY

A Compendium
of Traditional Catholic Prayers
and Practices

John A. F. Sill, Sr.

acta

IN THIS TIME OF MERCY
A Compendium of Traditional Catholic Prayers and Practices
By John A. F. Sill, Sr.

Editing by Patricia A. Lynch
Design and typesetting by Harvest Graphics
Copyright © 2016 by John A. F. Sill, Sr.

Published by ACTA Publications, 4848 N. Clark Saint, Chicago, IL 60640
(800) 397-2282, actapublications.com

All rights reserved. No part of this publication may be reproduced or transmitted in any form or by any means, electronic, digital, or mechanical, including photocopying and recording, or by any information storage and retrieval system, including the Internet, without permission from the publisher. Permission is hereby given to use short excerpts with proper citation in reviews and marketing copy, newsletters, church bulletins, class handouts, and scholarly papers.

Excerpts from the *Diary of Saint Maria Faustina Kowalski: Divine Mercy in My Soul,* © 1987 by Marian Fathers of the Immaculate Conception. "Prayer of Miraculous Trust" from *Into the Whirlwind,* © by Charles Johnston. *Rosary Novenas to Our Lady, including the Mysteries of Light* by Charles V. Lacey, revised by Gregory F. Augustine Pierce, © 2003 by ACTA Publications. "Simple Examination of Conscience, from *The Forgiveness Book,* © 2008 by Alice Camille and Paul Boudreau. Published by ACTA Publications. Scripture quotes from the *New Revised Standard Version of the Bible,* © 1989 by the Division of Christian Education of the National Council of the Churches of Christ in the USA. All used with permission. All rights reserved. All other prayers and texts have been taken from a variety of print and online media and are assumed to be in the public domain. Any claims of copyright should be addressed to the publisher.

Library of Congress Number: 2016930184
ISBN: 978-087946-569-8 (paperback)
ISBN: 978-087946-570-4 (hardcover)
Printed in the United States of America by Total Printing Systems
Year 25 24 23 22 21 20 19 18 17 16
Printing 12 11 10 9 8 7 6 5 4 3 2 First

♻ Text printed on 30% post-consumer recycled paper

TABLE OF CONTENTS

Foreword 5
Introduction 7
Traditional Catholic Prayers 13
Daily Prayers 29
The Rosary 39
The Mass 51
The Sacrament of Reconciliation 57
Stations of the Cross 73
Six Popular Devotions and Sacramentals 91
    The Brown Scapular 93
    Our Lady of Fatima 94
    The Seven Sorrows of Mary 99
    The Sacred Heart of Jesus 102
    The Miraculous Medal 110
    The Divine Mercy 111
A Year of Novenas, Prayers, and Observances 115
    January through December 117
    Lent through Corpus Christi 186
    Rosary Novena to Our Lady 203
Works of Mercy and Other Guidelines 223
Record of Prayer for the Dead 231
Notes 239
Index 247

FOREWORD

The rich young man in Matthew 19 asks Jesus the all-important question: "How do I possess everlasting life?" He tells Jesus that he has kept the commandments, but wonders "What do I need to do further?" Jesus responds that if the young man wishes to be perfect, he should sell all his possessions and give to the poor. Only then can the rich young man do as Jesus requests: "Come and follow me."

Following Jesus today means seeking spiritual perfection in your relationship with him, increasing your love for him day by day. Wouldn't you want to get an A-plus in your relationship with Jesus? A *summa cum laude* when you are received into heaven? Well, then, this prayer book, compiled and arranged with great care by John Sill, will help you increase your love for our Lord, discern God's will for you, lead a holy life, and over time achieve spiritual perfection.

I love the author's section on daily prayers and how to integrate those prayers into the rhythm of each day — morning, noon, and evening. The book is interactive, inviting personalization throughout and providing space for notes and reflections.

Saint Paul tells us, "So, whether you eat or drink, or whatever you do, do everything for the glory of God" (1 Corinthians 10:31). This book can help you give God the glory and live in ways as pleasing as incense that rises up towards heaven.

Reverend James Martell, Pastor
Holy Rosary Catholic Church
Memphis, Tennessee

I asked the Lord Jesus how he could tolerate so many sins and crimes and not punish them; the Lord answered me, "I have eternity for punishing [these], and so I am prolonging the time of mercy for the sake of [sinners]. But woe to them if they do not recognize this time of My visitation." (Diary of Saint Maria Faustina Kowalska, 1160)

∼

Prayer is a door that opens up into the mystery of God and at the same time a means of communing with him. It actuates the personal relationship with the Lord present in the very depths of spirituality. Prayer is the gate of entry to the center of the castle — God's dwelling place in the soul — where he sits upon his throne as King. (Saint Teresa of Jesus)

INTRODUCTION

I came to know God's mercy in profound ways as I made my way back to the Catholic Church after a thirteen-year absence. My heart was opened one weekend during a Methodist-sponsored Emmaus Walk, a program modeled on the Cursillo. Within a year, I made my confession at Holy Rosary Catholic Church in Memphis, Tennessee, experiencing what Jesus said to Saint Maria Faustina about "the time of mercy." As I became reacquainted with my Catholic faith, I was drawn to lead a devout and holy life.

Holy Rosary Parish provides a variety of free pamphlets, cards, and booklets on a table in the vestibule. Topics include how to make a good confession, how to pray the Rosary, and information on devotions. I collected some of the many resources I discovered there and purchased a prayer book at a local Catholic bookstore, but I found the resources and prayer book did not meet my needs. I still had to supplement my collection with other pamphlets and prayer cards. I finally realized that the only way to have a complete book would be to compose my own. This book is the result of my efforts over the course of several years and is printed with the guidance of Greg Pierce of ACTA Publications, whose *Rosary Novenas to Our Lady* is included here.

How to Use This Book

As you open this book, you may ask, "Where do I start?" You might begin with **Traditional Catholic Prayers**. You may already know many of these prayers by heart, but others may be less familiar. Memorization is a good practice, allowing the prayers to be accessible whenever the need arises and freeing your mind to enter more deeply into the meaning of the prayers.

You may decide to establish a prayer routine by using the selections in **Daily Prayers**. The daily schedule from the Roman Breviary calls for six hours of prayer: dawn or first rising (6:00 a.m.); morning; noon; afternoon (3:00 p.m.), dusk or evening (6:00 p.m.), and bedtime. With persistence, determination, and adaptation to your particular situation, you can face the challenges of beginning and remaining faithful to such a routine. Distractions and other obstacles are inevitable. If you have a smart phone, you might consider downloading a scheduling app to remind you of the times for prayer. I have found this helpful in my own practice.

During my return to the Church, I discovered new ways to pray popular devotions, including the Rosary, Stations of the Cross, and novenas. These are included in several sections. I took particular care in arranging **A Year of Novenas, Prayers, and Observances**. While some of the prayers are specific to certain days or seasons, most can be incorporated into your daily routine. For example, the Stations of the Cross are associated with Lent and the Feast of All Souls, but can be prayed whenever the need or desire arises. The Rosary, of course, is part of the daily routine of many Catholics.

I also have included detailed sections on the Mass — the central prayer of our Catholic tradition — and the Sacrament of Reconciliation.

An ample appendix includes a treasure trove of Catholic teaching, including the Precepts of the Church, Works of Mercy,

Virtues, and Fruits of the Spirit. I find it helpful to review this material on a regular basis, usually on the first Friday of each month. I also have provided space for you to record additional prayers, your personal goals, and your reflections, as well as a page for you to list the names of the dead for whom you pray.

I hope you discover, as I have, that God's mercy is poured out on all who wait on him. With Saint Teresa of Jesus, I hope you discover that prayer is "a door that opens up into the mystery of God."

> John A. F. Sill, Sr.
> Memphis, Tennessee
> January 1, 2016
> Solemnity of Mary, Mother of God,
> in the Jubilee Year of Mercy

DEDICATION

To the Holy Spirit

∽

*To my wife Anne who provided
loving support and encouragement*

TRADITIONAL CATHOLIC PRAYERS

The Bible, the writings of the early Church, and the words of holy men and women throughout the ages, including the saints, have given us a rich tradition of prayer. The prayers in this section are central to Catholic belief and practice and are worthy of memorization.

SIGN OF THE CROSS

The Sign of the Cross is made with the right hand touching the forehead at the word "Father," the chest at the word "Son," and the left and right shoulders at the words "Holy Spirit."

In the name of the Father, and of the Son,
and of the Holy Spirit. Amen.

OUR FATHER

Our Father, who are in heaven,
hallowed be your name,
Your kingdom come,
your will be done on earth as it is in heaven.
Give us this day our daily bread,
and forgive us our trespasses
as we forgive those who trespass against us.
And lead us not into temptation
but deliver us from evil. Amen.

HAIL MARY

Hail Mary, full of grace,
the Lord is with you.
Blessed are you among women,
and blessed is the fruit of your womb, Jesus.
Holy Mary, Mother of God,
pray for us sinners,
now and at the hour of our death. Amen.

GLORY BE

Glory be to the Father and to the Son and to the Holy Spirit,
as it was in the beginning, is now, and ever shall be,
world without end. Amen.

THE APOSTLES' CREED

I believe in God, the Father Almighty,
Creator of heaven and earth.
And in Jesus Christ, his only Son, our Lord,
who was conceived by the Holy Spirit,
born of the Virgin Mary,
suffered under Pontius Pilate,
was crucified, died, and was buried.
He descended into hell;
the third day he rose again from the dead;
he ascended into heaven,
and sits at the right hand of God the Father almighty;
from thence he will come to judge the living and the dead.

I believe in the Holy Spirit,
the holy catholic church,
the communion of saints,
the forgiveness of sins,
the resurrection of the body,
and life everlasting.
Amen.

ACT OF CONTRITION

O my God, I am heartily sorry for having offended you, and I detest all my sins, because I dread the loss of heaven and the pains of hell, but most of all because they offend you, my God, who are all good and deserving of all my love. I firmly resolve, with the help of your grace, to sin no more, and to avoid the near occasion of sin. Amen.

ACT OF FAITH

O my God, I firmly believe that you are one God in three divine Persons, the Father, the Son, and the Holy Spirit. I believe that your divine Son became man, died for our sins, and that he will come to judge the living and the dead. I believe these and all the truths that the holy Catholic Church teaches, because you have revealed them, who can neither deceive nor be deceived. Amen.

ACT OF HOPE

O my God, relying on your infinite goodness and promises, I hope to obtain pardon for my sins, the help of your grace, and life everlasting through the merits of Jesus Christ, my Lord and Redeemer. Amen.

ACT OF CHARITY

O my God, I love you above all things, with my whole heart and soul, because you are all good and worthy of all love. I love my neighbor as myself for the love of you. I forgive all who have injured me and ask pardon of all whom I have injured. Amen.

THE CONFITEOR

I confess to almighty God and to you, my brothers and sisters, that I have greatly sinned, in my thoughts and in my words, in what I have done and in what I have failed to do, through my fault, through my fault, through my most grievous fault. Therefore I ask blessed Mary Ever-Virgin, all the angels and saints, and you, my brothers and sisters, to pray for me to the Lord our God. Amen.

JESUS PRAYER

Lord Jesus, Son of God, have mercy on me, a sinner.

THE ANGELUS

The Angelus is to be recited three times a day — dawn, noon, and evening — except during the Easter season when the Regina Caeli is offered. See page 20.

V. The Angel of the Lord declared to Mary:
R. And she conceived of the Holy Spirit.

Hail Mary.... Amen.

V. Behold the handmaid of the Lord:
R. Be it done unto me according to your word.

Hail Mary.... Amen.

V. And the Word was made flesh:
R. And dwelled among us.

Hail Mary.... Amen.

Pray for us, O Holy Mother of God, that we may be made worthy of the promises of Christ.

Let us pray: Pour forth, we beseech you, O Lord, your grace into our hearts; that we, to whom the incarnation of Christ, your Son, was made known to us by the message of an angel, may by his Passion and Cross be brought to the glory of his Resurrection, through the same Christ our Lord. Amen.

THE REGINA CÆLI (QUEEN OF HEAVEN)

The Regina Caeli is recited instead of the Angelus during the Easter Season. See page 19.

Rejoice, O Queen of Heaven, Alleluia!
For he whom you did merit to bear, Alleluia!
Has risen as he said, Alleluia!
Pray for us to God, Alleluia!

V. Rejoice and be glad, O Virgin Mary, Alleluia!
R. For the Lord has risen indeed, Alleluia!

Let us pray: O God, who has given joy to the whole world through the Resurrection of your Son, our Lord Jesus Christ, grant that through the prayers of his Virgin Mother Mary we may obtain the joys of everlasting life. Through the same Christ our Lord. Amen.

HAIL, HOLY QUEEN

This prayer is offered after reciting five decades of the Rosary.

Hail, Holy Queen, Mother of mercy, our life, our sweetness, and our hope. To you do we cry, poor banished children of Eve; to you do we send up our sighs, mourning and weeping in this valley of tears. Turn, then, most gracious advocate, your eyes of mercy towards us; and after this our exile, show unto us the blessed fruit of your womb, Jesus.

O clement, O loving, O sweet Virgin Mary.

V. Pray for us, O holy Mother of God.
R. That we may be made worthy of the promises of Christ.

O God! whose only begotten Son, by his life, death, and resurrection, has purchased for us the reward of eternal life, grant, we beseech you, that, meditating upon these mysteries of the most holy Rosary of the Blessed Virgin Mary, we may imitate what they contain and obtain what they promise. Through the same Christ our Lord. Amen.

V. May the Divine assistance always remain with us.
R. And may the souls of all of the faithful departed, through the mercy of God, rest in peace. Amen.

PRAYER TO SAINT MICHAEL

Saint Michael the Archangel, defend us in the day of battle; be our safeguard against the wickedness and the snares of the Devil. May God rebuke him, we humbly pray, and do you, O Prince of the Heavenly Host, by the power of God, cast into hell Satan and all the other evil spirits who prowl through the world, seeking the ruin of souls. Amen.

PRAYER TO SAINT JOSEPH, THE WORKER

O glorious Saint Joseph, model of all those who are devoted to labor, obtain for me the grace to work conscientiously, putting the call of duty above my natural inclinations; to work with gratitude and joy in a spirit of penance for the remission of my sins, considering it an honor to employ and develop by means of labor the gifts received from God; to work with order, peace, moderation, and patience, without ever shrinking from weariness and difficulties; to work above all with purity of intention and detachment from self, having always death before my eyes and the account that I must render of time lost, of talents wasted, of good omitted, of vain complacency in success, so fatal to the work of God.

All for Jesus, all through Mary, all after your example, O Patriarch, Saint Joseph. Such shall be my watch-word in life and in death. Amen.

PRAYER BEFORE A CRUCIFIX

Behold, O kind and most sweet Jesus, I cast myself upon my knees in your sight, and with the most fervent desire of my soul I pray and beseech you that you would impress upon my heart lively sentiments of faith, hope, and charity; with true repentance for my sins and a firm desire of amendment, while with deep affection and grief of soul I ponder within myself and mentally contemplate your five most precious wounds, having before my eyes that which the Prophet David spoke of you, O good Jesus: "They have pierced my hands and my feet; they have numbered all my bones." Amen.

PRECIOUS BLOOD OFFERING

Immaculate Heart of Mary, do offer to the Eternal Father the Precious Blood of our Lord Jesus Christ, for the conversion of sinners, especially for *[name]*.

MEMORARE

Remember, O most gracious Virgin Mary, that never was it known that anyone who fled to your protection, implored your help, or sought your intercession was left unaided. Inspired with this confidence, I fly to you, O Virgin of virgins, my Mother; to you do I come; before you I stand, sinful and sorrowful. O Mother of the Word Incarnate, despise not my petitions, but in your mercy hear and answer me. Amen.

PRAYER OF THANKS

O God, of whose mercies there is no number and of whose goodness the treasure is infinite, we render thanks to your most gracious majesty for the gifts you have bestowed upon us, evermore beseeching your clemency, that as you grant the petitions of those who ask you, you will never forsake them, but will prepare them for the reward to come. Through Christ our Lord. Amen.

THE NAME OF JESUS

In honor of all the angels, in honor of my Guardian Angel,
to perform perfect penance, say:
Jesus, Jesus, Jesus…

In weak health, call on Jesus, stating the problem and saying:
Jesus, Jesus, Jesus…

For souls in Purgatory, say:
Jesus, Jesus, Jesus…

To thank God, say:
Jesus, Jesus, Jesus…

To defend against the Devil, in all dangers,
in all temptations, say:
Jesus, Jesus, Jesus…

THE SERENITY PRAYER

God grant me the serenity
To accept the things I cannot change;
Courage to change the things I can;
And wisdom to know the difference.

Living one day at a time;
Enjoying one moment at a time;
Accepting hardships as the pathway to peace;
Taking, as he did, this sinful world
As it is, not as I would have it;
Trusting that he will make all things right

If I surrender to his will;
So that I may be reasonably happy in this life
And supremely happy with him
Forever and ever in the next.
Amen.

PRAYER OF MIRACULOUS TRUST

Offer this prayer to help you turn things over to God, trusting that once you have done so, whatever he then allows is for your eternal good and that of those you love. Offering the prayer one time only for a particular intention is a practice of abandonment to trust.

Begin by asking for the help of Our Lady of Tepeyac, then make the Sign of the Cross and say:

By the power of our Lord, Jesus Christ; to the honor of Our Lady, the Immaculate Conception; in service to her Immaculate Heart; I ask you Lord *[state your intention here and ask for the intercession of the saint of your choice.]*.

I thank you for hearing my prayer. Your will be done. Amen.

Make the Sign of the Cross again, and give your intention over to God entirely with trust.

GRACE BEFORE MEALS

Traditional

Bless us, O Lord, and these your gifts that we are about to receive from your bounty, through Christ our Lord. Amen.

Advent

Father, as we prepare to celebrate the birth of your Son, prepare our hearts to receive him today and every day of our lives. You have blessed us with many wonderful things. As you nourish us with these gifts of the earth, nourish us further so that we may be effective witnesses of gospel life. We ask this through Christ our Lord. Amen.

Christmas

Father, the good news of our Savior's birth was announced first to the poor shepherds. As we give you thanks for the fruits of the earth, make us aware of the cries of those who are poor and in need. We ask this through Christ our Lord. Amen.

Lent

Father, through this season of penance grant that we may be true pilgrims and strangers in this world. As we give thanks for the gifts of creation, strengthen us through our sharing in this meal, that we may be nourished on our journey of repentance and conversion. We ask this through Christ our Lord. Amen.

Easter

Blessed are you, Lord our God. Your Son's Easter greeting to us is: "Peace be with you." As we offer you praise and thanks for this food, may we live out our thanks by being instruments of your peace. We ask this through Christ our Lord. Amen.

Pentecost

Father, the gift of the Holy Spirit fills the Church with joy. It is this same Spirit who gathers us together to praise your name in Jesus our Lord. As we share this meal, we ask that the Holy Spirit consume our lives in the fire of your love. May you be blessed and praised, now and forever. Amen.

Ordinary Time

Father, as we gather to enjoy these gifts, fill us with the spirit of thanksgiving so that we may offer you praise and thanks in sharing this meal. May you be blessed now and forever. Amen.

Father, all good things are of your making. As we share these gifts of creation, make us aware of your constant presence in our lives. We ask this through Christ our Lord. Amen.

Father, you call us together at this table and provide nourishment for us. May this food give us strength in mind and body so that we may do your work more effectively. We ask this through Christ our Lord. Amen.

GRACE AFTER MEALS

We give you thanks, almighty God, for these and all your blessings. You live and reign forever and ever. Amen.

DAILY PRAYERS

DAWN

Pray at 6:00 a.m. or upon rising.

We give thanks to God as our Creator and praise the masterpiece of his creation: Mary, the beloved daughter of God the Father, the First Person of the Blessed Trinity.

The Angelus or Regina Cæli

See pages 19-20. The Regina Caeli is prayed instead of the Angelus from Easter through Pentecost.

Other Prayers for This Time of Day

List the prayers you would like to include in your rising prayers.

_____

_____

_____

_____

_____

_____

_____

_____

_____

_____

_____

_____

MORNING

Pray before starting work or your daily routine.

The Daily Offering to the Sacred Heart of Jesus

O Jesus, through the Immaculate Heart of Mary, I offer you my prayers, works, joys, and suffering of this day in union with the Holy Sacrifice of the Mass throughout the world. I offer them for all the intentions of your Sacred Heart: the salvation of souls, reparation for sins, the reunion of all Christians; I offer them for the intentions of our Bishops and of all Apostles of Prayer and in particular for those recommended by our Holy Father this month.

Prayer to the Immaculate Heart of Mary

O most blessed mother, heart of love, heart of mercy, ever listening, caring, consoling, hear our prayer. As your children, we implore your intercession with Jesus your son.

Received with understanding and compassion the petitions we place before you today, especially *[your petitions]*.

We are comforted in knowing your heart is ever open to those who ask for your prayer.

We trust to your gentle care and intercession, those whom we love and who are sick or lonely or hurting. Help all of us, Holy Mother to bear our burdens in this life until we may share eternal life and peace with God forever. Amen.

Other Prayers for This Time of Day

List the prayers you would like to include in your morning prayers.

MIDDAY

Pray at noon or when the sun reaches its zenith.

We give thanks to God as our Redeemer, and praise the first one to be redeemed: Mary, the admirable Mother of God the Son, the Second Person of the Blessed Trinity.

The Angelus or Regina Cæli

See pages 19-20. The Regina Caeli is prayed instead of the Angelus from Easter through Pentecost.

Other Prayers for This Time of Day

List the prayers you would like to include in your midday prayers.

_____
_____
_____
_____
_____
_____
_____
_____
_____
_____
_____
_____

AFTERNOON

Pray at 3 p.m., the Hour of Mercy. See also page 112.

Hour of Mercy

You expired, Lord Jesus, but the source of life gushed forth for souls and the ocean of mercy opened upon the whole world. O Fount of life, unfathomable Divine Mercy, envelop the whole world and empty yourself out upon us.

Other Prayers for This Time of Day

List the prayers you would like to include in your afternoon prayers.

EVENING

Pray at 6:00 p.m. or at twilight.

We give thanks to God as our Savior, and praise the greatest one to be saved, who is already body and soul in heaven: Mary, the faithful spouse of God the Holy Spirit, the Third Person of the Blessed Trinity.

The Angelus or Regina Cæli

See pages 19-20. The Regina Caeli is prayed instead of the Angelus from Easter through Pentecost.

Other Prayers for This Time of Day

List the prayers you would like to include in your evening prayers.

_____
_____
_____
_____
_____
_____
_____
_____
_____
_____
_____
_____

BEDTIME PRAYERS

Review the actions of your day, identify your sins, and say an Act of Contrition. See page 17.

Other Prayers for This Time of Day

List the prayers you would like to include in your bedtime prayers.

SUBJECTS FOR DAILY MEDITATION

God to glorify
Jesus to imitate
The angels and saints to invoke
A soul to save
A body to honor
Sins to expiate
Virtues to acquire
Hell to avoid
Heaven to gain
Eternity to prepare for
Time to profit by
Neighbors to edify
The world to despise
Devils to combat
Passions to subdue
Death perhaps to suffer
And judgment to undergo

THE ROSARY

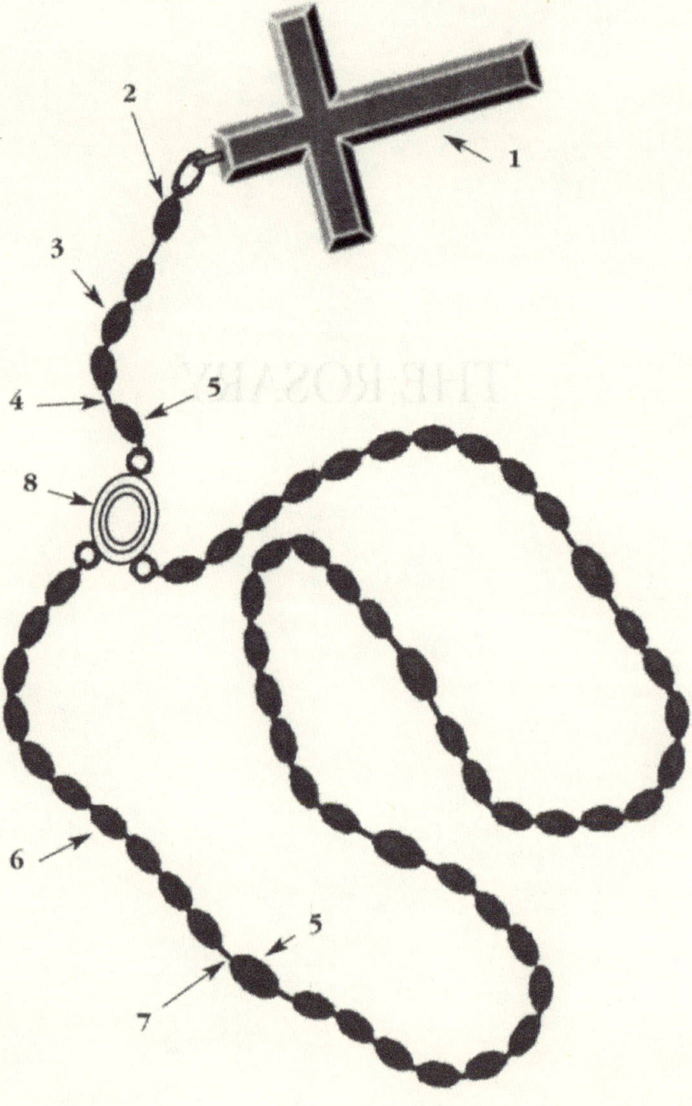
2
1
3
4
5
8
6
5
7

PRAYING THE ROSARY

There are four sets of Mysteries of the Rosary. Each set of Mysteries has five decades, during which we meditate on a particular event in the life of Jesus or his mother, Mary. The traditional three sets of Mysteries are the Joyful, Sorrowful, and Glorious Mysteries. Saint John Paul II suggested the addition of a fourth set of Mysteries, which he called the Mysteries of Light or the Luminous Mysteries, that focus on Jesus' public ministry. The four sets of Mysteries are meant to be prayed in chronological order of their subject matter, that is: Joyful, Luminous, Sorrowful, Glorious. Some people, especially on retreat or other important occasions, pray all four sets of Mysteries together or over a single day or short time period. Most people however, say one set of Mysteries at a time, often once a day. In this case, the four sets of Mysteries may be prayed in the intended order or may be said on certain days of the week, as noted in the description of each set of Mysteries on the pages that follow. Finally, at the end of each decade, those with special devotion to Our Lady of Fatima add the short "Decade Prayer," which is optional. Begin each recitation of the Rosary with the following prayers. (Numbers refer to the Rosary diagram on the previous page.)

Begin each recitation of the Rosary with the following prayers. Numbers refer to the Rosary diagram:

1. Sign of the Cross and Apostles' Creed
2. Our Father
3. Three Hail Marys
4. Glory Be

After announcing the Mystery and reading the associated Scripture passage, pray:

    5. *Our Father (large bead)*
    6. *Ten Hail Marys (small beads)*
    7. *Glory Be and Decade Prayer (space after last small bead)*

DECADE PRAYER

Oh my Jesus, forgive us our sins and save us from the fires of hell. Lead all souls to heaven, especially those most in need of your mercy.

    8. *Conclude each Rosary with the Hail, Holy Queen. See page 20.*

THE JOYFUL MYSTERIES

The Joyful Mysteries are marked by the joy radiating from the event of the Incarnation. This is clear from the very first mystery, the Annunciation, where Gabriel's greeting to the Virgin of Nazareth is linked to an invitation to messianic joy: "Rejoice, Mary." The whole of salvation…had led up to this greeting. (Apostolic Letter, "The Rosary of the Virgin Mary," Saint John Paul II)

~

These mysteries are traditionally prayed on Mondays and Saturdays, optionally on Sundays during Advent and Christmas Season.

First Joyful Mystery
The Annunciation
Fruit of the Mystery: Humility

And the angel came to her and said, "Greetings, favored one! The Lord is with you. Blessed are you among women" (Luke 1:28).

Second Joyful Mystery
The Visitation
Fruit of the Mystery: Charity

Elizabeth was filled with the Holy Spirit and exclaimed with a loud cry, "Blessed are you among women, and blessed is the fruit of your womb"(Luke 1:41-42).

Third Joyful Mystery
The Nativity
Fruit of the Mystery: Detachment from the World

She gave birth to her first-born son and wrapped him in bands of cloth, and laid him in a manger, because there was no place for them in the inn (Luke 2:7).

Fourth Joyful Mystery
The Presentation
Fruit of the Mystery: Purity

When the time came for their purification according to the law of Moses, they took him up to Jerusalem to present him to the Lord (as it is written in the law of the Lord, "Every first-born male shall be designated as holy to the Lord" (Luke 2:22-23).

Fifth Joyful Mystery
The Finding of the Child Jesus in the Temple
Fruit of the Mystery: Obedience to the Will of God

After three days they found him in the Temple, sitting among the teachers, listening to them and asking them questions. (Luke 2:46).

THE LUMINOUS MYSTERIES

Moving on from the infancy and hidden life in Nazareth to the public life of Jesus, our contemplation brings us to those mysteries which may be called in a special way "mysteries of light." Certainly, the whole mystery of Christ is a mystery of light. He is the "Light of the world" (John 8:12). Yet this truth emerges in a special way during the years of his public life. (Apostolic Letter, "The Rosary of the Virgin Mary," Saint John Paul II)

~

These mysteries are traditionally prayed on Thursdays.

First Luminous Mystery
The Baptism of Jesus in the Jordan River
Fruit of the Mystery: Giving Good Example

And when Jesus had been baptized…suddenly the heavens were opened to him and he saw the Spirit of God descending like a dove and alighting on him. And a voice from heaven, said "This is my Son, the Beloved with whom I am well pleased" (Matthew 3:16-17).

Second Luminous Mystery
The Wedding of Cana, the First Miracle of Jesus
Fruit of the Mystery: Responding to the Needs of Others

His mother said to the servants, "Do whatever he tells you".… Jesus said to them, "Fill the jars with water." And they filled them up to the brim (John 2:5-7).

Third Luminous Mystery
The Proclamation of the Kingdom of God
Fruit of the Mystery: Working for Social Justice

"And as you go, proclaim the good news, the kingdom of heaven has come near. Cure the sick, raise the dead, cleanse the lepers, cast out demons. You received without payment, give without payment" (Matthew 10:7-8).

Fourth Luminous Mystery
The Transfiguration
Fruit of the Mystery: Listening to the Word of God

And while he was praying, the appearance of his face changed and his clothes became dazzling white.... Then from the cloud came a voice that said, "This is my Son, my chosen, listen to him!" (Luke 9:29, 35).

Fifth Luminous Mystery
Institution of the Eucharist
Fruit of the Mystery: Helping to Build the Faith Community

Then he took a loaf of bread, and when he had given thanks, he broke it and gave it to them, saying, "This is my body, which is given for you."... And he did the same with the cup after supper, saying, "This cup that is poured out for you is the new covenant in my blood" (Luke 22:19-20)

THE SORROWFUL MYSTERIES

The Gospels give great prominence to the Sorrowful Mysteries of Christ. From the beginning, Christian piety, especially during the Lenten devotion of the Way of the Cross, has focused on the individual moments of the Passion, realizing that here is found the culmination of the revelation of God's love and the source of our salvation. (Apostolic Letter, "The Rosary of the Virgin Mary," Saint John Paul II)

These mysteries are traditionally prayed on Tuesday and Fridays, optionally on Sundays during Lent.

First Sorrowful Mystery
The Agony in the Garden
Fruit of the Mystery: Resignation to the Will of God

In his anguish he prayed more earnestly, and his sweat became like drops of blood falling down on the ground. When he got up from prayer, he came to his disciples, only to find them asleep, exhausted with grief (Luke 22:44-45).

Second Sorrowful Mystery
The Scourging at the Pillar
Fruit of the Mystery: Forbearance

Then Pilate took Jesus and had him flogged (John 19:1).

Third Sorrowful Mystery
The Crowning with Thorns
Fruit of the Mystery: Forgiveness

They stripped him and put a scarlet robe on him, And after twisting some thorns into a crown, they put it on his head. They put a reed in his right hand and knelt before him and mocked him (Matthew 27:28-29).

Fourth Sorrowful Mystery
The Carrying of the Cross
Fruit of the Mystery: Patience in Adversity

Carrying the cross by himself, he went out to what is called The Place of the Skull, which in Hebrew is called Golgotha (John 19:17).

Fifth Sorrowful Mystery
The Crucifixion
Fruit of the Mystery: Love of Our Enemies

And then Jesus, crying with a loud voice, said, "Father, into your hands I commend my spirit." Having said this, he breathed his last (Luke 23:46).

THE GLORIOUS MYSTERIES

"The contemplation of Christ's face cannot stop at the image of the Crucified One. He is the Risen One!" The Rosary has always expressed this knowledge born of faith and invited the believer to pass beyond the darkness of the Passion in order to gaze upon Christ's glory in the Resurrection and Ascension.... Mary herself would be raised to that same glory in the Assumption. (Apostolic Letter, "The Rosary of the Virgin Mary," Saint John Paul II)

∽

These mysteries are traditionally prayed on Wednesdays and Sundays.

First Glorious Mystery
The Resurrection
Fruit of the Mystery: Faith

"Do not be alarmed; you are looking for Jesus of Nazareth, he who was crucified. He has been raised; he is not here. Look, there is the place they laid him" (Mark 16:6).

Second Glorious Mystery
The Ascension
Fruit of the Mystery: Hope

So then the Lord Jesus, after he had spoken to them, was taken up into heaven and sat at the right hand of God (Mark 16:19).

Third Glorious Mystery
The Descent of the Holy Spirit
Fruit of the Mystery: Charity

All of them were filled with the Holy Spirit and began to speak in other languages, as the Spirit gave them ability (Acts 2:4).

Fourth Glorious Mystery
The Assumption of Our Blessed Mother into Heaven
Fruit of the Mystery: Union with Christ

"You are the glory of Jerusalem, you are the great pride of our nation.... You have done great good to Israel, and God is well pleased with it. May the Almighty Lord bless you forever " (Judith 15:9-10).

Fifth Glorious Mystery
The Coronation of Our Blessed Mother, Queen of Heaven
Fruit of the Mystery: Devotion to Mary

A great portent appeared in heaven: a woman clothed with the sun, with the moon under her feet, and on her head a crown of twelve stars (Revelation 12:1).

THE MASS

THE MASS

Holy Mass is a prayer itself, even the highest prayer that exists. It is the sacrifice, dedicated by our Redeemer at the Cross, and repeated every day on the altar. If you wish to hear Mass as it should be heard, you must follow with eye, heart, and mouth all that happens at the altar. Further, you must pray with the Priest the holy words said by him in the Name of Christ and which Christ says by him. You have to associate your heart with the holy feelings which are contained in these words and in this manner you ought to follow all that happens at the altar. When acting in this way, you have prayed Holy Mass. (Saint Pius X)

PREPARATION FOR MASS

The Eucharistic Fast

- *Water may be taken at any time.*
- *Solid food and drink may be taken up to one hour before Holy Communion. For the sick and aged and those who tend them, solid food and drink may be taken up to a quarter of an hour before.*
- *Those with prescribed medicines and those who are sick (not necessarily bed-ridden) may also take genuine medicines, solid or liquid, as well as non-alcoholic drinks, at any time before Holy Communion.*

Arrive at church early enough to accomplish a proper preparation for assisting at Holy Mass by having the fourfold intention of adoration, praise and thanksgiving, reparation, and entreaty. You can offer the Mass in union with the priest for some particular end.

BEFORE MASS

Pray the Our Father, Hail Mary, and Glory Be. Then conduct an Examination of Conscience and say an Act of Contrition. (See pages 17 and 59.)

DURING MASS

When the Priest offers the Host, pray silently:

I place, upon the paten my heart, the hearts of all those near and dear to me, especially the hearts of my relatives; the hearts of all those for whom I have promised to pray; the hearts of all those who have injured me; the hearts of all those whom I may have injured; the hearts of all the agonizing. Jesus, when you change the bread and wine into your Body and Blood, change our hearts into hearts pleasing to you.

When the Priest offers the Chalice, pray silently:
I place within the chalice the souls of all my relatives for whom I should pray; the souls of those for whom I may have forgotten to pray; the souls most devout to the Sacred Heart and the Blessed Virgin; the souls of the most abandoned. Jesus, when you change the wine into your Precious Blood, change these poor souls from their place of suffering into Eternal Happiness.

When the Priest elevates the Host and then the Chalice, pray silently the Fatima Eucharistic Prayer:

Most Holy Trinity, I adore you! My God, my God, I love you in the Most Blessed Sacrament.

Before communion, offer silently this prayer of Saint Thomas Aquinas:

Almighty and ever-living God, I approach the sacrament of your only-begotten Son, our Lord Jesus Christ. I come sick to the doctor of Life, unclean to the fountain of mercy, blind to the radiance of eternal light, and poor and needy to the Lord of heaven and earth. Lord, in your great generosity, heal my sickness, wash away my defilement, enlighten my blindness, enrich my poverty, and clothe my nakedness. May I receive the bread of angels, the King of kings and the Lord of lords, with humble reverence, purity and faith, repentance and love, and the determined purpose that will help to bring me to salvation. May I receive the sacrament of the Lord's body and blood, and its reality and power. Kind God, may I receive the body of your only begotten Son, our Lord Jesus Christ, born from the womb of the Virgin Mary, and so be received into his mystical body and numbered among his members. Loving Father, as on my earthly pilgrimage I now receive your beloved Son under the veil of a sacrament, may I one day see him face to face in glory, who lives and reigns with you forever. Amen.

After communion, offer another prayer of Saint Thomas Aquinas:

Lord, Father all-powerful and ever-living God, I thank you, for — even though I am a sinner, your unprofitable servant, not because of my worth but in the kindness of your mercy — you have fed me with the precious body and blood of your Son, our Lord Jesus Christ. I pray that this Holy Communion may not bring me condemnation and punishment but forgiveness and salvation. May it be a helmet of faith and a shield of good will. May it purify me from evil ways and put an end to my evil passions. May it bring me charity and patience, humility and obedience, and growth in the power to do good. May it be my strong defense against all my enemies, visible and invisible, and the perfect calming of all my evil impulses, bodily and spiritual. May it unite me more closely to you, the one true God, and lead me safely through death to everlasting happiness with you. And I pray that you will lead me, a sinner, to the banquet where you, with your Son and the Holy Spirit, are true and perfect light, total fulfillment, everlasting joy, gladness without end, and perfect happiness to your saints. Grant this through Christ our Lord. Amen.

After Mass, pray three Hail Marys, the Hail Holy Queen, the Prayer to Saint Michael, and the following prayer three times.

PRAYER TO THE SACRED HEART

Most Sacred Heart of Jesus. Have mercy upon us.

THE SACRAMENT OF RECONCILIATION

Before approaching a priest for the Sacrament of Reconciliation, reflect that this confession may be the last of your life. Therefore, prepare yourself for it as if you were lying sick upon your deathbed and already at the brink of the grave. Ask God to give you the grace to make a good examination of conscience, the light to see your sins clearly, and the strength to make a sincere confession and to amend your life.

Begin by examining yourself on your last confession.

1. *Did I forget a mortal sin through want of proper examination, or conceal or disguise it through shame?*
2. *Did I confess without true sorrow and a firm purpose of amendment?*
3. *Have I repaired all evil done to my neighbor?*
4. *Did I perform my penance without voluntary distractions?*
5. *Have I neglected my confessor's counsel, or fallen once again into habitual sins?*

Then examine yourself using the lists below.

IDENTIFY MORTAL SINS

Three simultaneous conditions must be fulfilled for a mortal sin:

1. *The act must be something very serious.*
2. *You must have sufficient understanding that what is being done is wrong.*
3. *You must have sufficient freedom of will.*

So you cannot commit a mortal sin if the matter is not serious, or if you did not know what you were doing, or if you did not act with full freedom.

NINE WAYS OF BEING ACCESSORY TO ANOTHER'S SIN

- By counsel
- By command
- By consent
- By provocation
- By praise or flattery
- By concealment
- By partaking
- By silence
- By defense of the ill done

SIMPLE EXAMINATION OF CONSCIENCE (Sample)

- Do I have a grateful heart, and do I give thanks for the gifts God has given me?
- Do I care for God's poor?
- Am I a peacemaker in my relationships and in my politics?
- Do I take time to pray and grow in my understanding of the way of Jesus, my Lord?
- Have I let go of past injuries and resentments?
- Do I treat my neighbor as I would want to be treated?
- Do I live a moral life of integrity and fidelity?
- Am I a good steward of my abilities and talents, and do I place them at the service of the Gospel?
- Do I stand up for justice, no matter what the personal cost?
- Am I free of the spirit of greed, possessiveness, and selfishness?
- Do I have confidence in the forgiveness of sin, and do I forgive others as I know myself to be forgiven?

- Is my faith alive, and do I witness to it so that others may know that I am a follower of Jesus Christ?
- Am I faithful to the vocations to which I have been called (parent, spouse, son, daughter, coworker, employer, employee, friend, neighbor, citizen, etc.)?
- Is there any condition of brokenness in my life that needs to be healed or reconciled?
- Is there any aspect of my present life that I must forsake in order to more deeply pursue the way of holiness?

THOROUGH EXAMINATION OF CONSCIENCE (Sample)

The First Commandment

I am the L ORD your God: you shall not have strange gods before me.

- Have I performed my duties towards God reluctantly or grudgingly?
- Did I recite my usual prayers?
- Did I receive Holy Communion in the state of mortal sin or without the necessary preparation?
- Did I break the one-hour Eucharistic fast?
- Did I fail to mention some grave sin in my previous confessions?
- Did I seriously believe in superstition or engage in superstitious practices (for example, fortune-telling, horoscopes)?
- Did I entertain serious doubt in matters of faith?

- Did I put my faith in danger by reading books, pamphlets, magazines, or blogs that contain doctrinal errors or encourage behavior contrary to Catholic faith and morals?
- Did I endanger my faith by joining or attending meetings and activities of organizations whose beliefs or goals are antithetical to the teachings of the Church or to the Catholic faith?
- Have I committed the sin of sacrilege (profanation of a sacred person, place, or thing)?

The Second Commandment

You shall not take the name of the LORD your God in vain.

- Did I try my best to fulfill the promises and resolutions that I have made to God?
- Did I make use of God's name mockingly, jokingly, angrily, or in any other irreverent manner?
- Did I make use of the Blessed Virgin Mary's name or the saints' names mockingly, jokingly, angrily, or in any other irreverent manner?
- Have I failed to give good example to others as a faithful member of the Catholic Church?
- Did I tell a lie under oath?
- Did I break (private or public) vows?

The Third Commandment
Remember to keep holy the LORD's Day.

- Did I miss Mass on Sundays or holy days of obligation?
- Did I allow myself to be distracted during Mass by not paying attention, looking around out of curiosity, etc.?
- Have I arrived at Mass so late without sufficient reason that I failed to fulfill a Sunday or holy day obligation?
- Did I misbehave in church, have improper posture or dress, or distract others?
- Did I generously help the Church meet her financial necessities or other needs to the extent that I am able?
- Did I fast and abstain on the days prescribed by the Church?
- Have I done or demanded servile work of others on Sundays or holy days of obligation that could have been done at another time?

The Fourth Commandment
Honor your father and your mother.

- Have I honored my parents (or their memory) by all my actions?
- Have I neglected to teach my own children their prayers, send them to church, or give them a Christian education?
- Have I given my children bad example at home, work, community, or church?

- Did I neglect to watch over my children: the companions they have, the books they read, the movies and TV shows they watch, their use of the Internet?
- Have I seen to it that my children received the sacraments (at appropriate ages)?

The Fifth Commandment

You shall not kill.

- Did I easily get angry or lose my temper?
- Was I envious or jealous of others?
- Did I injure or threaten the life of anyone? (For example, was I ever reckless in driving?)
- Was I an occasion of sin for others? Did I try to repair the scandal I caused to them?
- Have I actively lead others into sin?
- Did I neglect my health? Did I contemplate taking my own life?
- Have I intentionally physically or psychologically harmed myself or another?
- Did I get drunk or take prohibited drugs?
- Did I eat or drink more than a reasonable amount, allowing myself to get carried away by gluttony?
- Did I participate in or support the use of any form of physical violence?
- Did I consent or actively take part in any act preventing, ending, or not supporting human life?
- Did I cause anyone harm with my words or actions?
- Did I desire revenge or harbor enmity, hatred, or ill-feelings?

- Did I ask pardon whenever I offended anyone?
- Did I insult or tease others in mean-spirited or hurtful ways?

The Sixth and Ninth Commandments

You shall not commit adultery.
You shall not covet your neighbor's wife.

- Did I entertain indecent or impure thoughts?
- Did I consent to evil desires against the virtue of purity, even though I may not have carried them out? Were there any circumstances that aggravated the sin?
- Did I start or engage in sexually-degrading conversations?
- Did I seek out forms of entertainment (pornography) that put me in proximate occasion of sin?
- Did I follow the Catholic standards of modesty and decency that are safeguards of purity?
- Before going to a show or reading a book, did I try to find out its moral implications?
- Did I lead others to sins of impurity or immodesty?
- Did I commit impure acts by myself or with people of the same or opposite sex? Was there any circumstance of relationship, affinity, etc., that could have given the sin special gravity? Did these illicit relationships have any consequences for others? Did I do anything to prevent those consequences?
- Did I make improper use of marriage? Did I deprive my spouse of his or her marital rights? Did I betray conjugal fidelity in desire or in deed?

The Seventh and Tenth Commandments

You shall not steal.
You shall not covet your neighbor's goods.

- Did I steal any object or money? Did I give it back or do I have the intention to do so?
- Have I done or caused damage to others' property? Have I made or offered to make restitution?
- Did I harm anyone by deception, fraud, or coercion in business contracts or transactions?
- Did I spend beyond my means? Did I spend too much money unnecessarily due to whim, vanity, or caprice?
- Did I give contributions or donations to those in need according to my financial capacity?
- Was I envious of my neighbor's goods?
- Did I neglect to pay my debts?
- Did I retain anything found or stolen?
- Did I desire to steal?
- Was I diligent in my work and studies, or did I give in to laziness or love of comfort?
- Was I greedy? Did I exhibit an excessively materialistic view of life?

The Eighth Commandment

You shall not bear false witness against your neighbor.

- Did I tell lies? Did I repair any damage that may have resulted as a consequence of my failure to tell the truth?
- Have I unjustly accused others?

- Did I sin by detraction, that is, telling the faults of others without necessity?
- Did I sin by calumny, that is, telling derogatory lies about others?
- Did I engage in gossip, back-biting, or embarrassing tale-telling?
- Did I judge others rashly or suspected others falsely?
- Did I reveal secrets without due cause?

Faith

- Did I make an honest effort to grow in the virtue of faith by daily mental prayer on the mysteries of the faith as revealed in the life of Jesus Christ?
- Did I make at least a short act of faith every day?
- Did I pray daily for an increase of faith?
- Did I ever tempt God by relying on my own strength to cope with the trials in my life?
- Did I uncritically read or listen to those who oppose or belittle what I know are truths of my Catholic faith?
- What have I done today to externally profess my faith?
- Have I allowed the opinion of others to keep me from giving expression to my faith?
- Did I make a serious effort to resolve difficulties in myself that may have arisen about my faith?
- Did I ever defend my faith, prudently and charitably, when someone says something contrary to what I know is the teaching of the Church?
- Have I failed to help others overcome difficult questions they might have about the Catholic faith?

Hope

- Did I immediately say a short prayer when I found myself getting discouraged?
- Did I daily say a short act of hope?
- Did I dwell on my worries instead of dismissing them from my mind?
- Did I fail in the virtue of hope by my attachment to the things of this world?
- Did I try to see God's providence in everything that happens in my life?
- Did I try to see everything from the viewpoint of eternity?
- Was I confident that, with God's grace, I will be saved?
- Did I allow myself to worry about my past life and thus weaken my hope in God's mercy?
- Did I try to combine every fully deliberate action with at least a momentary prayer for divine help?
- How often have I complained, even internally?

Charity

- Have I told Jesus that I love him with my whole heart no matter what happens in my life?
- Have I accepted my trials, difficulties, and crosses with love?
- Did I see God's grace in every person I met?
- Have I failed in charity by speaking unkindly about others?
- Have I obsessed about what I considered someone's unkindness toward me?

- Is there someone I consciously avoid because I dislike that person? Did I fail to carry on a conversation with someone I find difficult to talk with?
- Have I been stubborn in asserting my own will?
- How thoughtful have I been in doing small favors for others? Have I allowed fatigue or bad moods to prevent me from being thoughtful of others?
- Have I focused on other people's weaknesses or faults?
- Have I failed to be cheerful in my dealings with others?
- Did I control my uncharitable thoughts as soon as they arise in my mind?
- Did I pray for others?
- Have I failed to give expressions of encouragement to others when given the opportunity?
- Have I controlled my emotions when someone irritated me?
- Have I failed to perform personal sacrifices or acts of kindness for others?

AFTER THE EXAMINATION OF CONSCIENCE

Having discovered the sins of which you have been guilty, together with their number, enormity, or such circumstances as may change their nature; you should endeavor to excite in yourself a heartfelt sorrow for having committed them and a sincere detestation of them, this being the most essential of all the dispositions requisite for a good confession. With what humility, fervor, and perseverance should you not importune the priest, who holds your heart in his hands to grant forgiveness to you!

Upon entering the confessional or reconciliation room, kneel or sit down and say:

Bless me, Father, for I have sinned.

Now tell the priest how long it has been since your last confession and begin to tell him your sins with a contrite and humble heart. After you have told your sins, end with the following:

For these and all the sins of my past life, especially my sin of *[name one grievous sin you have committed recently or in the past]* I am heartily sorry, beg pardon of God, and absolution from you, Father.

Listen with humility to the instruction of the priest.

Accept with submission the penance imposed, and if there is any reason you cannot fulfill that penance in a reasonable time, state this respectfully to the priest.

Then say the Act of Contrition:

O my God! I am heartily sorry for having offended you, and I detest all my sins, because I dread the loss of Heaven and the pains of hell, but most of all because they offend you, my God, who are all good and deserving of all my love. I firmly resolve, with the help of your grace, to confess my sins, to do penance, and to amend my life. Amen.

After the priest gives absolution, thank him and leave the confessional or reconciliation room. Make your way to a pew and say the prayers required for your penance.

STATIONS OF THE CROSS

Kneeling before the altar, make an Act of Contrition, and form the intention of gaining indulgences for yourself or for the souls in Purgatory.

PREPARATORY PRAYER

Most merciful Lord, with a contrite heart and penitent spirit I bow down before your divine Majesty. I adore you as my supreme Lord and Master, I believe in you, I hope in you, I love you above all things. I am heartily sorry for having offended you, my only and supreme God. I firmly resolve to amend my life; and although I am unworthy to obtain mercy, yet looking upon your holy Cross I am filled with peace and consolation. I will, therefore, meditate on your sufferings and visit the Stations in company with your sorrowful Mother and my holy Guardian Angel to promote your honor and to save my soul.

I desire to gain all indulgences granted to this holy exercise for myself and for the souls in Purgatory.

O Loving Jesus, inflame my cold heart with your love, that I may perform this devotion as perfectly as possible, and that I may live and die in union with you. Amen.

FIRST STATION
JESUS IS CONDEMNED TO DEATH

V. We adore you, O Christ, and we praise you.
R. Because by your holy Cross, you have redeemed the world.

Jesus, the most innocent of beings, is condemned to death, yes, to the shameful death of the Cross. In order to remain a friend of Caesar, Pilate delivers Jesus into the hands of his enemies. O fearful crime, to condemn Innocence to death and to displease God in order to please mere humans.

O innocent Jesus, I have sinned and I am guilty of eternal death; but that I may live, you do gladly accept the unjust sentence of death. For whom then shall I henceforth live if not for you, my Lord? If I desire to please others, I cannot be your servant. Let me, therefore, rather displease the whole world than not please you, O Jesus!

Pray an Our Father, Hail Mary, and Glory Be.

V. Lord Jesus, crucified.
R. Have mercy on us.

Pray or sing the Stabat Mater:

Through her heart, his sorrow sharing,
All his bitter anguish bearing,
Now at length the sword had passed.

SECOND STATION
JESUS CARRIES HIS CROSS

V. We adore you, O Christ, and we praise you.
R. Because by your holy Cross, you have redeemed the world.

When our divine Redeemer beheld the Cross, he most willingly reached out to it with his bleeding arms. He embraced it lovingly, kissed it tenderly, took it on his bruised shoulders and, exhausted as he was, carried it joyfully.

O my Jesus, I cannot be your friend and follower if I refuse to carry my cross. O beloved cross, I embrace you, I kiss you, I joyfully accept you from the hand of my God. Far be it from me to glory in anything save in the Cross of my Lord and Redeemer. By it the world shall be crucified to me, and I to the world, that I may be yours forever.

Pray an Our Father, Hail Mary, and Glory Be.

V. Lord Jesus, crucified.
R. Have mercy on us.

Pray or sing the Stabat Mater:

O, how sad and sore distressed
Was that Mother, highly blessed,
Of the sole begotten One!

THIRD STATION
JESUS FALLS THE FIRST TIME

V. We adore you, O Christ, and we praise you.
R. Because by your holy Cross, you have redeemed the world.

Carrying the Cross, our dear Savior was so weakened with its heavy weight that he fell exhausted to the ground. The Cross was light and sweet to him, but our sins made it so heavy and hard to carry.

Beloved Jesus, you did carry the burden and the heavy weight of my sins. Should I then not bear in union with you my light burden of suffering, and accept the sweet yoke of your commandments? Your yoke is sweet and your burden is light. I willingly accept it. I will take up my cross and follow you.

Pray an Our Father, Hail Mary, and Glory Be.

V. Lord Jesus, crucified.
R. Have mercy on us.

Pray or sing the Stabat Mater:

Christ above in torment hands:
She beneath beholds the pangs
Of her dying glorious Son.

FOURTH STATION
JESUS MEETS HIS BLESSED MOTHER

V. We adore you, O Christ, and we praise you.
R. Because by your holy Cross, you have redeemed the world.

How sad and how painful must it have been for Mary to behold her beloved Son laden with the Cross, covered with wounds and blood, and driven through the streets by savage executioners. What unspeakable pangs her most tender heart must have experienced. How earnestly did she desire to die instead of Jesus, or at least with him.

O Jesus, O Mary, I am the cause of the pains that pierced your hearts. Would that my heart might experience some of your sufferings. O Mother, let me share in thy sufferings and those of your Son, that I may obtain the grace of a happy death.

Pray an Our Father, Hail Mary, and Glory Be.

V. Lord Jesus, crucified.
R. Have mercy on us.

Pray or sing the Stabat Mater:

Is there one who would not weep,
Whelmed in miseries so deep,
Christ's dear Mother to behold?

FIFTH STATION
SIMON OF CYRENE HELPS JESUS CARRY HIS CROSS

V. We adore you, O Christ, and we praise you.
R. Because by your holy Cross, you have redeemed the world.

Simon of Cyrene was forced to help our exhausted Savior carry his Cross. How pleased would Jesus have been, had Simon offered his services of his own accord. However, Simon was not invited by Christ as we are. Jesus says: "Take up your cross and follow me." Nevertheless we recoil, and carry it grudgingly.

O Jesus, whosoever does not take up his cross and follow you, is not worthy of you. Behold, I cheerfully join you on the way of the Cross. I desire to carry it with all patience until death, that I may prove worthy of you.

Pray an Our Father, Hail Mary, and Glory Be.

V. Lord Jesus, crucified.
R. Have mercy on us.

Pray or sing the Stabat Mater:

Can the human heart refrain
From partaking in her pain,
In that Mother's pain untold?

SIXTH STATION
VERONICA WIPES THE FACE OF JESUS

V. We adore you, O Christ, and we praise you.
R. Because by your holy Cross, you have redeemed the world.

Moved by compassion, Veronica presents her veil to Jesus, to wipe his disfigured face. He imprints on it his holy countenance and returns it to her as a recompense. Shall Christ reward us in like manner? Then we too must do him a service. But we do a service to Christ every time we perform a work of mercy towards our neighbor, for Jesus says: "What you have done to the least of my brethren, you have done to me."

Dearest Jesus, what return shall I make you for all your benefits? Behold, I consecrate myself entirely to your service. My whole heart I give to you; stamp on it your holy image, that I may never forget you.

Pray an Our Father, Hail Mary, and Glory Be.

V. Lord Jesus, crucified.
R. Have mercy on us.

Pray or sing the Stabat Mater:

Bruised, derided, cursed, defiled,
She beheld her tender Child,
All with bloody scourges rent.

SEVENTH STATION
JESUS FALLS THE SECOND TIME

V. We adore you, O Christ, and we praise you.
R. Because by your holy Cross, you have redeemed the world.

Overwhelmed by the weight of the Cross, Jesus falls again to the ground. But the cruel executioners do not permit him to rest a moment. With thrusts and blows they urge him onward. With what cruelty Jesus is treated and trampled under foot. Remember, compassionate soul, that your sins caused Jesus this painful fall.

Have mercy on me, O Jesus, and help me never to fall into my former sins. From this moment I will strive sincerely never to sin again. But you, O Jesus, strengthen me with your grace, that I may faithfully carry out my resolution.

Pray an Our Father, Hail Mary, and Glory Be.

V. Lord Jesus, crucified.
R. Have mercy on us.

Pray or sing the Stabat Mater:

For the sins of his own nation,
Saw him hang in desolation
Till his spirit forth he sent.

EIGHTH STATION
JESUS SPEAKS TO THE WOMEN OF JERUSALEM

V. We adore you, O Christ, and we praise you.
R. Because by your holy Cross, you have redeemed the world.

Moved by compassion, these devoted women weep over our suffering Savior. But he turns to them and says: "Weep not for me, but weep for yourselves and your children. Weep for your sins and those of your children; for they are the cause of my suffering." We also must weep over our sins, for there is nothing more pleasing to our Lord and more useful to ourselves than the tears we shed out of contrition for our sins.

O Jesus, who shall give my eyes a torrent of tears, that I may day and night weep over my sins? I beseech you by your bitter and bloody tears to move my heart, so that tears may flow in abundance from my eyes and I may weep over your sufferings and over my sins until death.

Pray an Our Father, Hail Mary, and Glory Be.

V. Lord Jesus, crucified.
R. Have mercy on us.

Pray or sing the Stabat Mater:

O thou Mother: font of love!
Touch my spirit from above,
Make my heart with thine accord.

NINTH STATION
JESUS FALLS THE THIRD TIME

V. We adore you, O Christ, and we praise you.
R. Because by your holy Cross, you have redeemed the world.

Exhausted at the foot of Calvary, Jesus falls for the third time to the ground. How painfully must have been reopened all the wounds of his tender body by these repeated falls. And how enormous must our sins be, to cause Jesus to fall so painfully. Had not Jesus taken our sins upon himself, they would have plunged us into the abyss of Hell.

Most merciful Jesus, I return you a thousand thanks for not permitting me to die in my sins and fall into the abyss of Hell, as I have deserved so often. Enkindle in me a sincere desire to amend my life. Let me never again fall into sin, but grant me the grace of final perseverance.

Pray an Our Father, Hail Mary, and Glory Be.

V. Lord Jesus, crucified.
R. Have mercy on us.

Pray or sing the Stabat Mater:

Make me feel as thou has felt;
Make my soul to glow and melt,
With the love of Christ my Lord.

TENTH STATION
JESUS IS STRIPPED OF HIS GARMENTS

V. We adore you, O Christ, and we praise you.
R. Because by your holy Cross, you have redeemed the world.

Arriving on Calvary, Jesus was cruelly deprived of his garments. How painful the stripping must have been, because the garments adhered to his mangled body, so that in removing them parts of the flesh were torn away. Jesus is deprived of his garments that he may die possessed of nothing. How happy we are that we shall not die after laying aside our evil habits and tendencies.

Help me, O Jesus, to amend my life. Let it be renewed according to your will and desire. However painful the correction may be to me, I will not spare myself. With the assistance of your grace, I will refrain from all sinful pleasure and vain amusement, that I may die happy and live forever.

Pray an Our Father, Hail Mary, and Glory Be.

V. Lord Jesus, crucified.
R. Have mercy on us.

Pray or sing the Stabat Mater:

Holy Mother, pierce me through;
In my heart each wound renew
Of my Savior crucified.

ELEVENTH STATION
JESUS IS NAILED TO THE CROSS

V. We adore you, O Christ, and we praise you.
R. Because by your holy Cross, you have redeemed the world.

Stripped of his garments, Jesus is violently thrown down on the Cross. His hands and his feet are nailed to it in the most cruel way. Jesus remains silent, because it so pleases his heavenly Father. He suffers patiently, because he suffers for us. How do we act in sufferings and trials? How fretful and impatient, how full of complaints are we!

O Jesus, meek and patient Lamb, I renounce forever my impatience. Crucify, O Lord, my flesh, with its evil desires and vices. Punish and afflict me in this life, but spare me in the next. I resign myself altogether to your holy will. May it be done in all things.

Pray an Our Father, Hail Mary, and Glory Be.

V. Lord Jesus, crucified.
R. Have mercy on us.

Pray or sing the Stabat Mater:

Let me share with you his pain,
Who for all my sins was slain,
Who for me in torment died.

TWELFTH STATION
JESUS DIES ON THE CROSS

V. We adore you, O Christ, and we praise you.
R. Because by your holy Cross, you have redeemed the world.

Behold Jesus crucified! Behold his wounds received for love of us! His whole appearance betokens love. His head is bent to kiss us. His arms are extended to embrace us. His heart is open to receive us. Oh what love! Jesus dies on the Cross, to preserve us from eternal death.

Most lovable Jesus, who will grant that I may die for love of you? I will endeavor to die to the world and its vanities when I behold you on the Cross covered with wounds and crowned with thorns. Merciful Jesus, take me into your wounded heart, that I may despise all perishable things, to live and die for you alone.

Pray an Our Father, Hail Mary, and Glory Be.

V. Lord Jesus, crucified.
R. Have mercy on us.

Pray or sing the Stabat Mater:

Let me mingle tears with you,
Mourning him who mourned for me,
All the days that I may live.

THIRTEENTH STATION
JESUS IS TAKEN DOWN FROM THE CROSS

V. We adore you, O Christ, and we praise you.
R. Because by your holy Cross, you have redeemed the world.

Jesus did not descend from the Cross, but remained on it till his death. When taken down, he rested on the bosom of his beloved Mother as he had so often done in life. We, too, must persevere in our good resolutions, and do not flee from the cross. For whoever perseveres till the end shall be saved. Consider, moreover, how pure the heart should be that receives the body and blood of Jesus Christ in the adorable Sacrament of the Altar.

O Lord Jesus crucified, I most earnestly entreat you: Help me do what is right and let me not be separated from your Cross, for on it I desire to live and to die. Create in me, O Lord, a clean heart, that I may worthily receive you in Holy Communion, and that you may remain in me, and I in you, for all eternity.

Pray an Our Father, Hail Mary, and Glory Be.

V. Lord Jesus, crucified.
R. Have mercy on us.

Pray or sing the Stabat Mater:

By the cross with you to stay;
There with thee to weep and pray
Is all I ask of you to give.

FOURTEENTH STATION
JESUS IS LAID IN THE TOMB

V. We adore you, O Christ, and we praise you.
R. Because by your holy Cross, you have redeemed the world.

The body of Jesus is laid in a stranger's tomb. He who in this world had not whereon to rest his head would have no grave of his own after death. We whose hearts are still attached to this world must despise it that we may not perish with it.

O Jesus, you hast singled me out from the world, what then shall I seek in it? You have created me for Heaven, what then shall I desire upon earth? Depart from me, deceitful world, with thy vanities! Henceforth I will walk the way of the Cross traced out for me by my Redeemer and journey onward to my heavenly home, where my rest and my joy shall be forever.

Pray an Our Father, Hail Mary, and Glory Be.

V. Lord Jesus, crucified.
R. Have mercy on us.

Pray or sing the Stabat Mater:

Virgin of all virgins best,
Listen to my fond request:
Let me share your grief divine.

SIX POPULAR DEVOTIONS

THE BROWN SCAPULAR

Pope Paul VI wrote that we should "ever hold in great esteem the practices and exercises of the devotion to the most Blessed Virgin Mary that have been recommended for centuries by the Magisterium of the Church. And among them we judge well to recall especially the Marian Rosary and the religious use of the Scapular of Mount Carmel."

The Blessed Virgin appeared to Saint Simon Stock, Superior General of the Carmelite Order, on July 16, 1251, holding a brown scapular in her hand and giving this promise: "Take this scapular. It shall be a sign of salvation, a protection in danger, and a pledge of peace. Whosoever dies wearing this scapular shall not suffer eternal fire."

The Brown Scapular consists of two pieces of 100% brown wool, held together by two strings, ribbons, cords, or chains and placed over the head with the strings resting on the shoulders and one piece of cloth at the front and the other at the back.

Most Brown Scapulars have pictures on the two pieces of wool. Pictures are not necessary, but you wish to choose a scapular that has the image of the Sacred Heart. See page 103, promise 9.

Only a priest or an authorized ordained deacon may enroll someone in the Confraternity of the Brown Scapular.

Replacement scapulars do not need to be blessed because the blessing as well as the enrollment are attached to the enrollee for life. However, there is no harm in having a priest bless the new scapular.

OUR LADY OF FATIMA
DEVOTION OF THE FIVE FIRST SATURDAYS

In her six appearances to Lucia dos Santos, and Francisco and Jacinta Marto at Fatima in 1917, the Blessed Mother emphasized the necessity of praying the Rosary daily, wearing the Brown Scapular of Mount Carmel, and performing acts of reparation and sacrifice.

She also asked that the Faithful practice a new devotion of reparation on the first Saturday of five consecutive months called, "Devotion of The Five First Saturdays."

In October 1925 Lucia dos Santos was received as a postulant at the Dorothean house at Pontevedra, Spain. On December 10, 1925, Sister Lucy received an apparition in her convent cell of the Child Jesus and the Virgin Mary. The Holy Virgin showed her a Heart surrounded by thorns and said to her:

> *Look, my daughter, at my heart surrounded with thorns with which the ungrateful pierce at every moment by their blasphemies and ingratitude. You at least try to console me and announce in my name that I promise to assist at the moment of death, with all the graces necessary for salvation, all those who, on the first Saturday of five consecutive months shall confess, receive Holy Communion, recite five decades of the Rosary, and keep me company for fifteen minutes while meditating on the fifteen mysteries of the Rosary, with the intention of making reparation to me.*

Instructions for the conditions
regarding the First Saturdays of the month:

1. *Confess and receive Holy Communion*

   Confession may be made days preceding or following the first Saturday of each month, provided that Holy Communion is received in the state of grace. Should one forget to form the intention of making reparation to the Immaculate Heart of Mary, it may be formed at the first opportunity to go to confession.

2. *Recite the Rosary*

   Five decades of the Rosary may be recited at any time or place. Usually the Rosary is said before or after Mass. See page 41.

3. *"Keep me company for fifteen minutes while meditating on the mysteries of the Rosary."*

   An additional fifteen minutes of meditation is required on one or more mysteries. It may include all, but it is preferable to meditate on one mystery each month.

4. *All of the conditions mentioned above should be fulfilled with the intention of making reparation to the Immaculate Heart of Mary.*

First Five Saturdays

Five First Saturdays of reparation were requested to atone for the five ways in which people offend the Immaculate Heart of Mary:

1. *Attacks upon Mary's Immaculate Conception,*
2. *Attacks against her Perpetual Virginity,*
3. *Attacks upon her Divine Maternity and the refusal to accept her as the Mother of all humankind,*
4. *For those who try to publicly implant in children's hearts indifference, contempt, and even hatred of this Immaculate Mother,*
5. *For those who insult her directly in her sacred images.*

~

The greatest joy is to see the Immaculate Heart of our so tender Mother known, loved, and consoled by the means of this devotion. (Sister Lucia)

THE FATIMA PRAYERS

Eucharistic Prayer

Pray three times:

Most Holy Trinity, I adore you! My God, my God, I love you in the Most Blessed Sacrament.

Pardon Prayer

Pray three times:

My God, I believe, I adore, I hope, and I love you!
I ask pardon for those who do not believe,
do not adore, do not hope, and do not love you.

Decade Prayer

Recite after the Glory Be at the end of each decade of the Rosary.

O my Jesus, forgive us our sins, save us from the fire of Hell, lead all souls to Heaven, especially those who are most in need of your mercy.

Angel's Prayer

This prayer was given to the three children by the Angel who preceded Our Lady's first appearance to them. Pray three times.

Most Holy Trinity, Father, Son, and Holy Spirit, I adore you profoundly. I offer you the Most Precious Body, Blood, Soul, and Divinity of Jesus Christ, present in all the tabernacles of the world, in reparation for the outrages, sacrileges, and indifference by which he is offended. And through the infinite merit of his Most Sacred Heart and the Immaculate Heart of Mary, I beg of you the conversion of poor sinners.

Sacrifice Prayer

Our Lady of Fatima said, "Many souls go to Hell because there are none to sacrifice themselves and to pray for them." Both the Angel of Fatima and Our Lady asked for sacrifices for sinners, enjoined us: "Sacrifice yourself." We can begin by making small sacrifices each day, denying ourselves something, practicing patience, and engaging in a spiritual or corporal work of mercy, all as an offering for sinners and those in need of mercy.

The Angel of Fatima, also, told the three children to "Offer prayers and sacrifices constantly to the Most High.... Make of everything you can a sacrifice, and offer it to God as an act of reparation for the sins by which He is offended, and in supplication for the conversion of sinners.... Above all, accept and bear with submission the sufferings which the Lord will send you."

Pray these words from Our Lady of Fatima whenever you make a sacrifice or perform a work of mercy for the sake of sinners.

O Jesus, it is for love of you, for the conversion of sinners, and in reparation for the sins committed against the Immaculate Heart of Mary.

THE SEVEN SORROWS OF MARY

Saint Alphonsus Liguori testified to revelations given by our Lord to Saint Elizabeth of Hungary (1207-1231). In these revelations, Jesus promised four special graces to those dedicated to the sufferings of his Mother:

1. That those who, before death, invoke the Blessed Mother in the name of her sorrows should obtain true repentance of all their sins.
2. That he would protect in their tribulations all who remember this devotion, and that he would protect them especially at the hour of death.
3. That he would impress upon their minds the remembrance of his Passion, and that they should have their reward for it in Heaven.
4. That he would commit such devout souls to the hands of Mary, so that she might obtain for them all the graces she wanted to lavish upon them.

Our Lady also directly revealed to Saint Bridget of Sweden (1303-1373) the amazing graces granted by her Son for all those who daily pray seven Hail Marys while meditating on her seven sorrows and tears:

1. "I will grant peace to their families."
2. "They will be enlightened about the Divine Mysteries."
3. "I will console them in their pains, and I will accompany them in their work."

4. *"I will give them as much as they ask for as long as it does not oppose the adorable will of my Divine Son or the sanctification of their souls."*

5. *"I will defend them in their spiritual battles with the infernal enemy, and I will protect them at every instant of their lives."*

6. *"I will visibly help them at the moment of their death — they will see the face of their Mother."*

7. *"I have obtained this grace from my divine Son, that those who propagate this devotion to my tears and sorrows will be taken directly from this earthly life to eternal happiness, since all their sins will be forgiven and my Son will be their eternal consolation and joy."*

DEVOTION OF THE SEVEN SORROWS OF MARY

Pray one Hail Mary while meditating on each of the following Seven Sorrows of Mary.

1. *The prophecy of Simeon.*
2. *The flight of the Holy Family into Egypt.*
3. *The loss of the Child Jesus in the Temple.*
4. *Mary meeting Jesus carrying his Cross.*
5. *The Crucifixion.*
6. *Mary receiving the body of Jesus from the Cross.*
7. *The body of Jesus being placed in the tomb.*

Then pray three Hail Marys in remembrance of the tears Mary shed because of the suffering of her Divine Son.

Concluding Prayer

Pray for us, O Most Sorrowful Virgin, that we may be made worthy of the promises of Christ.

Lord Jesus, we now implore, both for the present and for the hour of our death, the intercession of the Most Blessed Virgin Mary, your Mother, whose Holy Soul was pierced during your Passion by a sword of grief. Grant us this favor, O Savior of the world, who lives and reigns with the Father and the Holy Spirit forever and ever. Amen.

THE SACRED HEART OF JESUS

Our present-day form of the devotion to the Sacred Heart of Jesus came from the visions of Saint Margaret Mary Alacoque (1647-1690), a nun from the Order of the Visitation of Holy Mary. She received several apparitions of Jesus Christ beginning on December 27, 1673, until the final one eighteen months later.

To gain the promises, we must:

1. *Receive Holy Communion on nine consecutive first Fridays.*
2. *Have the intention of honoring the Sacred Heart of Jesus and of reaching final perseverance.*
3. *Offer each Holy Communion as an act of atonement for offenses against the Blessed Sacrament.*

Honor the Sacred Heart of Jesus on the First Friday of each month with the following prayers,

1. *Act of Consecration to the Sacred Heart of Jesus*
2. *Act of Reparation*
3. *The Litany of the Sacred Heart of Jesus*
4. *Adoration of the Blessed Sacrament*

The Twelve Promises of the Sacred Heart of Jesus to Saint Margaret Mary Alacoque

In a spirit of reparation, faithful Catholics consecrate the First Friday of each month to the Sacred Heart.

1. I will give them all the graces necessary in their state of life.
2. I will establish peace in their families and will unite families that are divided.
3. I will comfort them in all their afflictions.
4. I will be their secure refuge during life, and above all in death.
5. I will bestow the blessings of Heaven on all their enterprises.
6. Sinners shall find in my Heart the source and the infinite ocean of mercy.
7. Tepid souls shall become fervent.
8. Fervent souls shall quickly mount to high perfection.
9. I will bless every place in which an image of my Heart shall be exposed and honored and will imprint my love on the hearts of all those who would wear this image on their person. I will also destroy in them all unruly inclinations.
10. I will give the priests who are animated by a tender devotion to my Divine Heart the gift of touching the most hardened hearts.
11. Those who promote this devotion shall have their names written in my Heart, never to be effaced.
12. I promise you in the excessive mercy of my Heart that my all-powerful love will grant to all those who receive comunion

on the first Friday on nine consecutive months the grace of final penitence; they shall not die in my disgrace nor without receiving their Sacraments. My divine Heart shall be their safe refuge in this last moment.

Prayer of Consecration to the Sacred Heart

I give myself and consecrate to the Sacred Heart of our Lord Jesus Christ, my person and my life, my actions, pains and sufferings, so that I may be unwilling to make use of any part of my being other than to honor, love, and glorify the Sacred Heart.

This is my unchanging purpose, namely, to be all his, and to do all things for the love of him, at the same time renouncing with all my heart whatever is displeasing to him.

I therefore take you, O Sacred Heart, to be the only object of my love, the guardian of my life, my assurance of salvation, the remedy of my weakness and inconstancy, the atonement for all the faults of my life and my sure refuge at the hour of death.

Be then, O Heart of goodness, my justification before God the Father, and turn away from me the strokes of his righteous anger. O Heart of love, I put all my confidence in you, for I fear everything from my own wickedness and frailty but hope for all things from your goodness and bounty.

Remove from me all that can displease you or resist your holy will; let your pure love imprint your image so deeply upon my heart that I shall never be able to forget you or to be separated from you. May I obtain from all your loving kindness the grace of having my name written in your Heart, for in you I desire to place all my happiness and glory, living and dying bound to you. Amen.

Act of Reparation

Sacred Heart of Jesus, animated with a desire to repair the outrages unceasingly offered to you, we prostrate before your throne of mercy and, in the name of all humankind, pledge our love and fidelity to you!

The more your mysteries are blasphemed, the more firmly we shall believe them, O Sacred Heart of Jesus!

The more impiety endeavors to extinguish our hopes of immortality, the more we shall trust in your Heart, sole hope of humankind!

The more hearts resist your Divine attractions, the more we shall love you, O infinitely amiable Heart of Jesus!

The more unbelief attacks your Divinity, the more humbly and profoundly we shall adore it, O Divine Heart of Jesus!

The more your holy laws are transgressed and ignored, the more we shall delight to observe them, O most holy Heart of Jesus!

The more your Sacraments are despised and abandoned, the more frequently we shall receive them with love and reverence, O most liberal Heart of Jesus!

The more the imitation of your virtues is neglected and forgotten, the more we shall endeavor to practice them, O Heart, model of every virtue!

The more the devil labors to destroy souls, the more we shall be inflamed with desire to save them, O Heart of Jesus, zealous lover of souls!

The more sin and impurity destroy the image of God in us, the more we shall try by purity of life to be a living temple of the Holy Spirit, O Heart of Jesus!

The more your Holy Church is despised, the more we shall endeavor to be her faithful children, O Sweet Heart of Jesus!

The more your vicar on earth is persecuted, the more we will honor him as the infallible head of your Holy Church, show our fidelity, and pray for him, O kingly Heart of Jesus!

O Sacred Heart, through your powerful grace, may we become your apostles in the midst of a corrupted world and be your crown in the kingdom of heaven. Amen.

Litany of the Sacred Heart

Lord, have mercy.

Christ, have mercy.

Lord, have mercy.

Redeemer of the world, have mercy on us.

God the Holy Spirit, have mercy on us.

Holy Trinity, One God, have mercy on us.

Heart of Jesus, Son of the Eternal Father, have mercy on us.

Heart of Jesus, formed by the Holy Spirit in the womb of the Virgin Mother, have mercy on us.

Heart of Jesus, substantially united to the Word of God, have mercy on us.

Heart of Jesus, of infinite majesty, have mercy on us.

Heart of Jesus, sacred temple of God, have mercy on us.

Heart of Jesus, tabernacle of the Most High, have mercy on us.

Heart of Jesus, house of God and gate of Heaven, have mercy on us.

Heart of Jesus, burning furnace of charity, have mercy on us.

Heart of Jesus, abode of justice and love, have mercy on us.

Heart of Jesus, full of goodness and love, have mercy on us.

Heart of Jesus, abyss of all virtues, have mercy on us.

Heart of Jesus, most worthy of all praise, have mercy on us.

Heart of Jesus, king and center of all hearts, have mercy on us.

Heart of Jesus, in whom dwells the fullness of divinity,
have mercy on us.

Heart of Jesus, in whom the Father was well pleased,
have mercy on us.

Heart of Jesus, desire of everlasting life, have mercy on us.

Heart of Jesus, patient and most merciful, have mercy on us.

Heart of Jesus, enriching all who invoke you,
have mercy on us.

Heart of Jesus, fountain of life and holiness,
have mercy on us.

Heart of Jesus, propitiation for our sins, have mercy on us.

Heart of Jesus loaded down with opprobrium,
have mercy on us.

Heart of Jesus, bruised for our offenses, have mercy on us.

Heart of Jesus, obedient to death, have mercy on us.

Heart of Jesus, pierced with a lance, have mercy on us.

Heart of Jesus, source of consolation, have mercy on us.

Heart of Jesus, our life and resurrection, have mercy on us.

Heart of Jesus, victim for our sins, have mercy on us.

Heart of Jesus, salvation for those who trust in you,
have mercy on us.

Heart of Jesus, hope of those who die in you,
have mercy on us.

Heart of Jesus, delight of all the saints, have mercy on us.

Lamb of God, who takes away the sins of the world,
spare us, O Lord.

Lamb of God, who takes away he sins of the world,
graciously hear us, O Lord.

Lamb of God, who takes away the sins of the world,
have mercy on us, O Lord.

V. Jesus, meek and humble of heart,
R. Make our own hearts like yours.

Let us pray. Almighty and eternal God, look upon the heart of your most beloved Son and upon the praises and satisfaction he offers you in the name of sinners; and to those who implore your mercy, in your great goodness grant forgiveness in the name of the same Jesus Christ, your Son, who lives and reigns with you forever and ever. Amen.

Adoration of the Blessed Sacrament

Listed below are some suggested things to do during the Hour of Adoration of the Blessed Sacrament in honoring the Sacred Heart of Jesus.

- *Pray the Rosary.*
- *Meditate using Scripture.*
- *Meditate using the one or more of the mysteries of the Rosary.*
- *Read about the life and pray the prayer of a saint important to you.*
- *Be in the presence of God by sitting quietly and listening.*
- *Pray for an intercession for someone.*
- *Recite a favorite prayer.*
- *Do any combination of the above.*

THE MIRACULOUS MEDAL
(MEDAL OF THE IMMACULATE CONCEPTION)

The Medal of the Immaculate Conception was requested by Saint Catherine Labouré, a Daughter of Charity, following her visions of the Blessed Virgin Mary in 1830. Mary asked her to take these images to her priest confessor, telling him that they should be put on medallions and that, "All those who wear it, when it is blessed, will receive great graces especially if they wear it round the neck. Those who repeat this prayer with devotion will be in a special manner under the protection of the Mother of God. Graces will be abundantly bestowed upon those who have confidence." The request was approved by Bishop Vachette two years later.

O Mary conceived without sin
pray for us who have recourse to you.

THE DIVINE MERCY

Our Lord first appeared to Saint Maria Faustina Kowalska in 1931, giving the following for the outpouring of his grace and mercy.

- Image of The Divine Mercy
- Divine Mercy Chaplet
- Hour of Mercy (3:00 p.m.)
- The Feast of The Divine Mercy
- Spreading the Honor of The Divine Mercy

Image of The Divine Mercy

> "I promise that the soul that will venerate this image will not perish. I also promise victory over [its] enemies already here on earth, especially at the hour of death. I myself will defend it as my own glory." (Diary of Saint Maria Faustina Kowalska, 48)

Divine Mercy Chaplet

Using a Rosary, make the Sign of the Cross with the crucifix.

Pray the following prayer on the first large bead.

You expired, Jesus, but the source of life gushed forth for souls, and the ocean of mercy opened up for the whole world. O Fount of Life, unfathomable Divine Mercy, envelop the whole world and empty yourself out upon us.

O Blood and Water, that gushed forth from the Heart of Jesus as a fountain of Mercy for us, I trust in you!

On the next three smaller beads, pray the Our Father, Hail Mary, and the Apostles' Creed.

On the remaining large beads before each decade, pray:

Eternal Father, I offer you the Body and Blood, Soul and Divinity of your dearly Beloved Son, our Lord Jesus Christ, in atonement for our sins and those of the whole world.

On the ten small beads of each decade, pray:

For the sake of his sorrowful Passion, have mercy on us and on the whole world.

Conclude with this prayer, repeated three times:

Holy God, Holy Mighty One, Holy Immortal One, have mercy on us and on the whole world.

Hour of Mercy

> *"At three o'clock, implore my mercy, especially for sinners; and, if only for a brief moment, immerse yourself in my Passion, particularly in my abandonment at the moment of agony. This is the hour of great mercy. In this hour, I will refuse nothing to the soul that makes a request of me in virtue of My Passion." (Diary of Saint Maria Faustina Kowalska, 1320)*

Feast of the Divine Mercy

The Novena of Chaplets to the Divine Mercy is a preparation for the Feast of The Divine Mercy on the Sunday after Easter. The novena begins on Good Friday. See page 187.

> *"On this day the very depths of my tender mercy are open. I pour out a whole ocean of graces upon those souls who approach the font of my mercy. The soul that will go to Confession and receive Holy Communion shall obtain complete forgiveness of sins and punishment. On that day all divine flood gates through which graces flow are opened. Let no soul fear to draw near to me, even though its sins be as scarlet." (Diary of Saint Maria Faustina Kowalska, 699)*

Spreading the Honor of The Divine Mercy

> *"Souls who spread the honor of my mercy I shield through their entire life as a tender mother her infant, and at the hour of death I will not be a Judge for them, but the Merciful Savior." (Diary of Saint Maria Faustina Kowalska, 1075)*

> *"I demand from you deeds of mercy, which are to arise out of love for me. You are to show mercy to your neighbors always and everywhere. You must not shrink from this or try to excuse or absolve yourself from it. I am giving you three ways of exercising mercy toward your neighbor: the first — by deed, the second — by word, the third — by prayer. In these three degrees is contained the fullness of mercy, and it is an unquestionable proof of love for me. By this means a soul glorifies and pays reverence to my Mercy." (Diary of Saint Maria Faustina Kowalska, 742)*

A YEAR OF NOVENAS, PRAYERS, AND OBSERVANCES

*The term novena derives from **novem**, the Latin word for **nine**. A novena usually consists of prayers for nine straight days, during which the faithful ask God for special graces. These prayers may be as simple as a daily recitation of the Rosary or short prayers throughout the day. Novenas may be dedicated to mourning; preparation for a liturgical feast, such as Christmas; a personal need, such as healing; or penance. This section includes twelve months of novenas as well as a listing of feast days and related prayers. Novenas and prayers for Lent, Easter, and Pentecost begin on page 186. Feast days listed here are from the Liturigcal Calendar for Dioceses of the United States.*

JANUARY

January 1 » Solemnity of Mary, Mother of God

Father, source of light in every age, the virgin conceived and bore your Son who is called Wonderful God, Prince of Peace. May her prayer, the gift of a mother's love, be your people's joy through all ages. May her response, born of a humble heart, draw your Spirit to rest on your people. Grant this through Christ our Lord. Amen.

Canticle of Mary (Magnificat)

My soul proclaims your greatness, O my God, and my spirit has rejoiced in you my Savior; for you have regarded me as your holy handmaid; henceforth all generations shall call me blessed; for you who are mighty have done great things for me, and Holy is your Name; your mercy is on those who fear you throughout all generations. You have showed strength with your arm. You have scattered the proud in the conceit of their heart. You have put down the mighty from their seat, and have lifted up the powerless. You have filled the hungry with good things, and have sent the rich away empty. Remembering your mercy, you have helped your people Israel as you promised Abraham and Sarah. Mercy to their children forever. Amen.

January 2 » Saints Basil the Great and Gregory Nazianzen

January 4 » Saint Elizabeth Ann Seton

January 5 » Saint John Neumann

January 6 » Saint André Bessette

January 8 » Our Lady of Prompt Succor

This novena is usually prayed January 7-15. "Succor" means "assistance and support in times of hardship or distress."

O Almighty and Eternal God, seeing us surrounded by so many dangers and miseries, grant in your infinite goodness that the Blessed Virgin Mary, Mother of your Divine Son, may defend us from the evil spirit, protect us from all adversities, obtain for us *[mention your request here]*, and safely guide us to the kingdom of Heaven. This we ask of you through our Lord Jesus Christ, your Son, who lives and reigns with you in the unity of the Holy Spirit, God, forever. Amen.

O Mary, Mother of God, amid the tribulations of the world, watch over the people of God and be to us truly Our Lady of Prompt Succor. Make haste to help us in all our necessities, that in this fleeting life you may be our succor. Obtain for us *[mention your request here]*. Help us to gain life everlasting through the merits of Jesus, your Son, our Lord and Redeemer. Amen.

Our Lady of Prompt Succor, hasten to help us.
Our Lady of Prompt Succor, hasten to help us.
Our Lady of Prompt Succor, hasten to help us.
Pray the Our Father, Hail Mary, and Glory Be.

Litany of Our Lady of Prompt Succor

Lord, have mercy.

Christ, have mercy.

Lord, have mercy.

Christ, hear us.

Christ, graciously hear us.

God the Father of Heaven, have mercy on us.

God the Son, Redeemer of the world, have mercy on us.

Holy Trinity, one God, have mercy on us.

Respond with "pray for us" to each of the following invocations.

Holy Mary...

Mother of the Infant Jesus…

Our Lady of Prompt Succor…

Our Lady of Prompt Succor
of all who invoke you with confidence…

Our Lady of Prompt Succor
of all who are devout toward the Infant Jesus…

Our Lady of Prompt Succor
for obtaining a lively faith…

Our Lady of Prompt Succor
for sustaining the hope of Christians…

Our Lady of Prompt Succor
for obtaining and persevering in charity…

Our Lady of Prompt Succor
for observing the law of God…

Our Lady of Prompt Succor
for observing perseverance in virtue and good works…

Our Lady of Prompt Succor
in every spiritual necessity…

Our Lady of Prompt Succor
against the revolt of self-will…

Our Lady of Prompt Succor
in the occasion of sin…

Our Lady of Prompt Succor
in every temptation…

Our Lady of Prompt Succor
against the evil spirit…

Our Lady of Prompt Succor
for obtaining contrition…

Our Lady of Prompt Succor
of those wishing to re-enter the path of salvation…

Our Lady of Prompt Succor
for the conversion of sinners…

Our Lady of Prompt Succor
in every temporal necessity…

Our Lady of Prompt Succor
in every affliction…

Our Lady of Prompt Succor
of afflicted families…

Our Lady of Prompt Succor
of the sick and the poor…

Our Lady of Prompt Succor
against contagious diseases and epidemics…

Our Lady of Prompt Succor
in every accident…

Our Lady of Prompt Succor
against destruction by fire…

Our Lady of Prompt Succor
against lightning and tempest…

Our Lady of Prompt Succor against destruction by flood …

Our Lady of Prompt Succor of travelers …

Our Lady of Prompt Succor of navigators …

Our Lady of Prompt Succor of the shipwrecked …

Our Lady of Prompt Succor against the enemies
of our country...

Our Lady of Prompt Succor in time of war...

Our Lady of Prompt Succor of those aspiring to the holy
priesthood and the religious life...

Our Lady of Prompt Succor of laborers
in the Lord's vineyard...

Our Lady of Prompt Succor of missionaries
who spread the faith...

Our Lady of Prompt Succor
for those searching for the faith...

Our Lady of Prompt Succor against
the enemies of the Church...

Our Lady of Prompt Succor at the hour of death...

Our Lady of Prompt Succor
for the deliverance of the Souls in Purgatory...

Lamb of God, who takes away the sins of the world,
spare us, O Lord.

Lamb of God, who takes away the sins of the world,
graciously hear us, O Lord.

Lamb of God, who takes away the sins of the world,
have mercy on us.

V: Our Lady of Prompt Succor, pray for us.
R: That we may be made worthy of the promises of Christ.

O Almighty and Eternal God, who sees us surrounded by so many dangers and miseries, grant in your infinite goodness that the Blessed Virgin Mary, Mother of your Divine Son, may defend us from the evil spirit and protect us against all adversities, that always and with prompt succor she may deliver us from every evil of soul and body, and safely guide us to the kingdom of Heaven, through the merits of our Lord Jesus Christ, your Son, who lives and reigns with you in the unity of the Holy Spirit, one God, world without end. Amen.

January 21 » Saint Agnes of Rome

January 22 or 23 » Day of Prayer
for the Legal Protection
of Unborn Children

Almighty God, our Father,
you who have given us life
and intended us to have it forever,
grant us your blessings.
Enlighten our minds to an awareness
and to a renewed conviction
that all human life is sacred
because it is created
in your image and likeness.
Help us to teach, by word
and the example of our lives,

that life occupies the first place,
that human life is precious,
because it is the gift of God
whose love is infinite.

Give us the strength to defend human life
against every influence
or action that threatens or weakens it,
as well as the strength
to make every life more human
in all its aspects.

Give us the grace...
when the sacredness of life
before birth is attacked,
to stand up and proclaim
that no one ever has the authority
to destroy unborn life.

Give us the grace...
when a child is described as a burden
or is looked upon only as a means
to satisfy an emotional need,
to stand up
and insist that every child is a unique
and unrepeatable gift of God,
a gift of God with a right to a loving
and united family.

Give us the grace...
when the institution of marriage

is abandoned to human selfishness
or reduced to a temporary conditional arrangement
that can easily be terminated,
to stand up and affirm
the indissolubility of the marriage bond.

Give us the grace…
when the value of the family is threatened
because of social and economic pressure,
to stand up and reaffirm
that the family is necessary
not only for the private good of every person,
but also for the common good of every society,
nation and state.

Give us the grace…
when freedom is used to dominate the weak,
to squander natural resources and energy,
to deny basic necessities to people,
to stand up and affirm
the demands of justice and social love.

Almighty Father,
give us courage to proclaim the supreme dignity
of all human life and to demand
that society itself give its protection.
We ask this in your name,
through the redemptive act
of your Son and in the Holy Spirit. Amen.

January 23 » Saints Marianne Cope of Moloka'i and Vincent of Saragossa

January 25 » Conversion of Saint Paul the Apostle

January 26 » Saints Timothy and Titus

January 28 » Saint Thomas Aquinas

Other Prayers and Observances in January

FEBRUARY

February 2 » Presentation of the Lord

February 3 » Saint Blaise

February 5 » Saint Agatha of Sicily

February 6 » Saint Paul Miki of Japan and Companions

February 11 » Our Lady of Lourdes

The novena is prayed February 2-10.

First Day: O Mary Immaculate, Our Lady of Lourdes, Virgin and Mother, Queen of Heaven, chosen from all eternity to be the Mother of the Eternal Word and in virtue of this title preserved from original sin, we kneel before you as did little Bernadette at Lourdes and pray with childlike trust in you that as we contemplate your glorious appearance at Lourdes, you will look with mercy on our present petition and secure for us a favorable answer to the request for which we are making this novena. *[Make your request.]* O brilliant star of purity, Mary Immaculate, Our Lady of Lourdes, glorious in your assumption, triumphant in your coronation, show unto us the mercy of the Mother of God, Virgin Mary, Queen and Mother, be our comfort, hope, strength, and consolation. Amen.

Our Lady of Lourdes, pray for us.
Saint Bernadette, pray for us.

Second Day: Be blessed, O most pure Virgin, for having vouchsafed to manifest yourself shining with light, sweetness and beauty, in the Grotto of Lourdes, saying to the child Saint Bernadette: "I am the Immaculate Conception!" O Mary Immaculate, inflame our hearts with one ray of the burning love of your pure heart. Let them be consumed with love for Jesus and for you, in order that we may merit one day to enjoy your glorious eternity. O dispenser of his graces here below, take into your keeping and present to your Divine Son the petition for which we are making this novena. *[Make your request.]* O brilliant star of purity, Mary Immaculate, Our Lady of Lourdes, glorious in your assumption, triumphant in your coronation, show unto us the mercy of the Mother of God, Virgin Mary, Queen and Mother, be our comfort, hope, strength, and consolation. Amen.

Our Lady of Lourdes, pray for us.
Saint Bernadette, pray for us.

Third Day: You are all fair, O Mary, and there is in you no stain of original sin. O Mary, conceived without sin, pray for us who have recourse to you. O brilliant star of sanctity, as on that lovely day, upon a rough rock in Lourdes you spoke to the child Bernadette and a fountain broke from the plain earth and miracles happened and the great shrine of Lourdes began, so now I beseech you to hear our fervent prayer and do, we beseech you, grant us the petition we now so earnestly seek. *[Make your request.]* O brilliant star of purity, Mary Immaculate, Our Lady of Lourdes, glorious in your assumption, triumphant in your coronation, show unto us the mercy of the Mother of God, Virgin Mary, Queen and Mother, be our comfort, hope, strength, and consolation. Amen.

Our Lady of Lourdes, pray for us.
Saint Bernadette, pray for us.

Fourth Day: O Immaculate Queen of Heaven, we your wayward, erring children join our unworthy prayers of praise and thanksgiving to those of the angels and saints and your own that the One, Holy, and Undivided Trinity may be glorified in heaven and on earth. Our Lady of Lourdes, as you looked down with love and mercy upon Bernadette as she prayed her Rosary in the grotto, look down now, we beseech you, with love and mercy upon us. From the abundance of graces granted you by your Divine Son, sweet Mother of God, give to each of us all that your motherly heart sees we need, and at this moment look with special favor on the grace we seek in this novena. *[Make your request.]* O brilliant star of purity, Mary Immaculate, Our Lady of Lourdes, glorious in your assumption, triumphant in your coronation, show unto us the mercy of the Mother of God, Virgin Mary, Queen and Mother, be our comfort, hope, strength, and consolation. Amen.

Our Lady of Lourdes, pray for us.
Saint Bernadette, pray for us.

Fifth Day: O Mary Immaculate, Mother of God and our mother, from the heights of your dignity look down mercifully upon us while we, full of confidence in your unbounded goodness and confident that your Divine Son will look favorably upon any request you make of him in our behalf, we beseech you to come to our aid and secure for us the favor we seek in this novena. *[Make your request.]* O brilliant star of purity, Mary Immaculate, Our Lady of Lourdes, glorious in your assumption, triumphant in your coronation, show unto us the mercy of the Mother of God, Virgin Mary, Queen and Mother, be our comfort, hope, strength, and consolation. Amen.

Our Lady of Lourdes, pray for us.
Saint Bernadette, pray for us.

Sixth Day: O glorious Mother of God, so powerful under your special title of Our Lady of Lourdes, to you we raise our hearts and hands to implore your powerful intercession in obtaining from the gracious Heart of Jesus all the help and graces necessary for our spiritual and temporal welfare and for the special favor we so earnestly seek in this novena. *[Make your request.]* O Lady of Bernadette, with the stars of heaven in your hair and the roses of earth at your feet, look with compassion upon us today as you did so long ago on Bernadette in the Grotto of Lourdes. O brilliant star of purity, Mary Immaculate, Our Lady of Lourdes, glorious in your assumption, triumphant in your coronation, show unto us the mercy of the Mother of God, Virgin Mary, Queen and Mother, be our comfort, hope, strength, and consolation. Amen.

Our Lady of Lourdes, pray for us.
Saint Bernadette, pray for us.

Seventh Day: O Almighty God, who by the Immaculate Conception of the Blessed Virgin Mary did prepare a worthy dwelling place for your Son, we humbly beseech you that as we contemplate the apparition of our Lady in the Grotto of Lourdes we may be blessed with health of mind and body. O most gracious Mother Mary, beloved Mother of our Lord and Redeemer, look with favor upon us as you did that day on Bernadette and intercede with him for us that the favor we now so earnestly seek may be granted to us. *[Make your request.]* O brilliant star of purity, Mary Immaculate, our Lady of Lourdes, glorious in your assumption, triumphant in your coronation, show unto us the mercy of the Mother of God, Virgin Mary, Queen and Mother, be our comfort, hope, strength, and consolation. Amen.

Our Lady of Lourdes, pray for us.
Saint Bernadette, pray for us.

Eighth Day: O Immaculate Mother of God, from heaven itself you came to appear to the little Bernadette in the rough Grotto of Lourdes. As Bernadette knelt at your feet and the magic spring burst forth, and as multitudes have knelt ever since before your shrine, O Mother of God, we kneel before you today to ask that in your mercy you plead with your Divine Son to grant the special favor we seek in this novena. *[Make your request.]* O brilliant star of purity, Mary Immaculate, Our Lady of Lourdes, glorious in your assumption, triumphant in your coronation, show unto us the mercy of the Mother of God, Virgin Mary, Queen and Mother, be our comfort, hope, strength, and consolation. Amen.

Our Lady of Lourdes, pray for us.
Saint Bernadette, pray for us.

Ninth Day: O glorious Mother of God, to you we raise our hearts and hands to implore your powerful intercession in obtaining from the benign Heart of Jesus all the graces necessary for our spiritual and temporal welfare, particularly for the grace of a happy death. O Mother of our Divine Lord, as we conclude this novena for the special favor we seek at this time *[make your request]*, we feel animated with confidence that your prayers on our behalf will be graciously heard. O Mother of our Lord, through the love you bear to Jesus Christ and for the glory of his Name, hear our prayers and obtain our petitions. O brilliant star of purity, Mary Immaculate, Our Lady of Lourdes, glorious in your assumption, triumphant in your coronation, show unto us the mercy of the Mother of God, Virgin Mary, Queen and Mother, be our comfort, hope, strength, and consolation. Amen.

Our Lady of Lourdes, pray for us.
Saint Bernadette, pray for us.

Litany of Our Lady of Lourdes

Lord, have mercy. / Lord, have mercy.

Christ, have mercy. / Christ, have mercy.

Lord, have mercy. / Lord, have mercy.

Christ, hear us. / Christ, graciously hear us.

God the Father of Heaven / have mercy on us.
God the Son, Redeemer of the world / have mercy on us.
God the Holy Spirit / have mercy on us.
Holy Trinity, one God / have mercy on us.

To each of the following invocations, respond "Pray for us."

Holy Mary…
Holy Mother of God…
Mother of Christ…
Mother of our Savior…

Our Lady of Lourdes, help of Christians…
Our Lady of Lourdes, source of love…
Our Lady of Lourdes, mother of the poor…
Our Lady of Lourdes, mother of the handicapped…
Our Lady of Lourdes, mother of orphans…
Our Lady of Lourdes, mother of all children…
Our Lady of Lourdes, mother of all nations…
Our Lady of Lourdes, mother of the Church…
Our Lady of Lourdes, friend of the lonely…
Our Lady of Lourdes, comforter of those who mourn…
Our Lady of Lourdes, shelter of the homeless…
Our Lady of Lourdes, guide of travelers…
Our Lady of Lourdes, strength of the weak…
Our Lady of Lourdes, refuge of sinners…

Our Lady of Lourdes, comforter of the suffering...
Our Lady of Lourdes, help of the dying...

Queen of heaven...

Queen of peace ...

Lamb of God, you take away the sins of the world / spare us, O Lord.

Lamb of God, you take away the sins of the world / hear us, O Lord.

Lamb of God, you take away the sins of the world / have mercy on us.

Christ, hear us. / Christ, graciously hear us.

Let us pray: Grant us, your servants, we pray you, Lord God, to enjoy perpetual health of mind and body. By the glorious intercession of Blessed Mary ever Virgin, may we be delivered from present sorrows, and enjoy everlasting happiness. Through Christ our Lord. Amen.

February 22 » The Chair of Saint Peter

Other Prayers and Observances in February

MARCH
March 3 » Saint Katharine Drexel

....

March 4 » Novena of Grace

The novena in honor of Saint Francis Xavier is offered March 4-12.

O Jesus, answer our petitions as we kneel before you. O Heart of Jesus, hear and grant our prayers. Pray for us, Saint Francis Xavier, that we may be made worthy of the promises of Christ.

Let us pray: Come, Holy Spirit, fill the hearts of your faithful. Enkindle in them the fire of your love. Send forth your spirit and they shall be created and you shalt renew the face of the earth.

Recite the Glory Be.

O most lovable and loving Saint Francis Xavier, in union with you I adore the Divine Majesty. The remembrance of the favors with which God blessed you during life and of your glory after death fills me with joy; and I unite with you in offering to God my humble tribute of thanksgiving and of praise. I implore you to secure for me through your powerful intercession the inestimable blessing of living and dying in the state of grace. I also beseech you to obtain for me the favor I ask in this novena. *[Mention your intentions.]* But if what I ask is not for the glory of God and for the good of my soul, do you obtain for me what is more conducive to both. Amen.

Recite the Our Father, Hail Mary, and Glory Be.

Pray for us, Saint Francis Xavier, that we may be made worthy of the promises of Christ.

March 19 » Saint Joseph

The novena to the spouse of the Blessed Virgin Mary is offered March 11–19.

O Saint Joseph, whose protection is so great, so strong, so prompt before the throne of God, I place in you all my interests and desires.

O Saint Joseph, assist me by your powerful intercession and obtain for me from your Divine Son all spiritual blessings through Jesus Christ our Lord, so that, having engaged here below your heavenly power, I may offer my thanksgiving and homage to the most loving of Fathers.

O Saint Joseph, I never weary contemplating you and Jesus asleep in your arms; I dare not approach while he reposes near your heart. Press him in my name and kiss his fine head for me, and ask him to return the kiss when I draw my dying breath. Amen.

O Saint Joseph, hear my prayers and obtain my petitions. O Saint Joseph, pray for me. *[Mention your intention.]*

Pray the Memorare. See page 23.

March 25 » The Annunciation of the Lord

This novena is offered March 16-25.

I greet you, Ever-Blessed Virgin, Mother of God, Throne of Grace, miracle of Almighty Power! I greet you, Sanctuary of the Most Holy Trinity and Queen of the Universe, Mother of Mercy and Refuge of Sinners!

Most loving Mother, attracted by your beauty and sweetness and by your tender compassion, I confidently turn to you, miserable as I am, and beg of you to obtain for me from your dear Son, the Savior.

I request in this novena: *[mention your request]*.

Obtain for me also, Queen of Heaven, the most lively contrition for my many sins and the grace to imitate closely those virtues you practiced so faithfully, especially humility, purity, and obedience. Above all, I beg you to be my Mother and Protectress, to receive me into the number of your devoted children, and to guide me from your high throne of glory.

Do not reject my petitions, Mother of Mercy! Have pity on me, and do not abandon me during life or at the moment of my death. Amen.

Other Prayers and Observances in March

APRIL

April 7 » Saint John Baptist de La Salle

April 11 » Saint Stanislaus

April 16 » Saint Bernadette of Lourdes

Saint Bernadette, chosen by Almighty God as a channel of his graces and blessings, through your humble obedience to the requests of our Blessed Mother, Mary, you gained for us the miraculous waters of spiritual and physical healing.

We implore you to listen to our pleading prayers that we may be healed of our spiritual and physical imperfections. Place our petitions in the hands of our Holy Mother, Mary, so that she may place them at the feet of her beloved Son, our Lord and Savior Jesus Christ, that he may look on us with mercy and compassion. *[Make your petition.]*

Help us, dear Saint Bernadette, to follow your example, so that irrespective of our own pain and suffering we may always be mindful of the needs of others, especially those whose sufferings are greater than ours. As we await the mercy of God, remind us to offer up our pain and suffering for the conversion of sinners and in reparation for the sins and blasphemies of mankind.

Pray for us, Saint Bernadette, that like you we may always be obedient to the will of our Heavenly Father, and that through our prayers and humility we may bring consolation to the

Most Sacred Heart of Jesus and the Immaculate Heart of Mary that have been so grievously wounded by our sins. Holy Saint Bernadette of Lourdes, pray for us. Amen.

April 25 » Saint Mark

April 29 » Saint Catherine of Siena

Other Prayers and Observances in April

MAY

May 2 » Saint Athanasius

May 10 » Saint Damien de Veuster of Moloka'i

....

May 13 » Our Lady of Fatima

This novena is prayed May 4-12. See also the Devotion of the First Five Saturdays, page 94.

Most Holy Virgin, who deigned to come to Fatima to reveal to the three little shepherds the treasures of graces hidden in the recitation of the Rosary, inspire our hearts with a sincere love of this devotion, so that by meditating on the mysteries of our redemption that are recalled in it, we may gather the fruits and obtain the conversion of sinners, the conversion of Russia, and this favor I so earnestly seek *[mention your request]* that I ask of you in this novena, for the greater Glory of God, for your own honor, and for the good of all people. Amen.

Pray three sets of the following prayers: Our Father, Hail Mary, and Glory Be.

....

May 14 » Saint Matthias

May 15 » Saint Isidore

May 24 » Mary, Help of Christians

May 26 » Saint Philip Neri

May 31 » The Visitation of the Blessed Virgin Mary

Other Prayers and Observances in May

JUNE

June 1 » Saint Justin Martyr

....

Early to Mid-June » Feast of the Sacred Heart

The Feast of the Sacred Heart is observed nineteen days after Pentecost with the nine-day novena ending on the evening before the feast.

Act of Reparation to the Sacred Heart of Jesus

O sweet Jesus, whose overflowing charity to us is returned on our part by so much forgetfulness, negligence, and contempt, behold us prostrate before your altar (in your presence) eager to repair by a special act of homage the cruel indifference and injuries to which your loving Heart is everywhere subject.

Mindful, alas, that we ourselves have had a share in such great indignities, that we now deplore from the depths of our hearts, we humbly ask your pardon and declare our readiness to atone by voluntary expiation not only for our own personal offenses but also for the sins of those who, straying for from the path of salvation, refuse in their obstinate infidelity to follow you, their Shepherd and Leader, or, renouncing the vows of their Baptism, have cast off the sweet yoke of your Law.

We are now resolved to expiate each and every deplorable outrage committed against you; we are determined to make amends for the manifold offenses against Christian modesty in unbecoming dress and behavior, for all the foul seductions laid to ensnare the feet of the innocent, for the frequent violations of Sundays and holidays, and the shocking blasphemies uttered against you and your saints. We wish also to make amends for the insults to which your vicar on Earth and your priests are subjected; for the profanation, by conscious neglect or terrible acts of sacrilege, of the very Sacrament of your Divine Love; and lastly for the public crimes of nations who resist the rights and teaching authority of the Church you have founded.

Would, O divine Jesus, we were able to wash away such abominations with our blood. We now offer, in reparation for these violations of your divine honor, the satisfaction you once made to your eternal Father on the cross and that you continue to renew daily on our altars; we offer it in union with the acts of atonement of your Virgin Mother and all the saints and of the pious faithful on earth; and we sincerely promise to make recompense, as far as we can with the help of your grace, for all neglect of your great love and for the sins we and others have committed in the past. Henceforth we will live a life of unwavering faith, of purity of conduct, of perfect observance of the precepts of the Gospel and especially that of charity. We promise to the best of our power to prevent others from offending you and to bring as many as possible to follow you.

O loving Jesus, through the intercession of the Blessed Virgin Mary, our model in reparation, deign to receive the voluntary offering we make of this act of expiation, and by the crowning gift of perseverance, keep us faithful unto death in our duty and the allegiance we owe to you, so that we may one day come to that happy home where you, with the Father and the Holy Spirit, live and reign, God, world without end. Amen.

Novena to the Sacred Heart of Jesus

O my Jesus, you have said: "Truly I say to you, ask and you will receive, seek and you will find, knock and it will be opened to you." Behold, I knock, I seek, and I ask for the grace of *[name your request here]*.

Pray an Our Father, Hail Mary, and Glory Be.

Sacred Heart of Jesus, I place all my trust in you.

O my Jesus, you have said: "Truly I say to you, if you ask anything of the Father in my name, he will give it to you." Behold, in your name, I ask the Father for the grace of *[name your request here]*.

Pray an Our Father, Hail Mary, and Glory Be.

Sacred Heart of Jesus, I place all my trust in you.

O my Jesus, you have said: "Truly I say to you, heaven and earth will pass away but my words will not pass away." Encouraged by your infallible words I now ask for the grace of *[name your request here]*.

Pray an Our Father, Hail Mary, and Glory Be.

Sacred Heart of Jesus, I place all my trust in you.

O Sacred Heart of Jesus, for whom it is impossible not to have compassion on the afflicted, have pity on us miserable sinners and grant us the grace we ask of you, through the Sorrowful and Immaculate Heart of Mary, your tender Mother and ours.

Pray the Hail, Holy Queen.

Saint Joseph, foster father of Jesus, pray for us. Amen.

June 11 » Saint Barnabas

June 13 » Saint Anthony of Padua

June 21 » Saint Aloysius Gonzaga

June 24 » The Nativity of Saint John the Baptist

June 27 » Our Mother of Perpetual Help

Pray the novena nine days before the feast or on nine consecutive Wednesdays.

See at your feet, O Mother of Perpetual Help, a poor sinner who has recourse to you and confides in you. O Mother of Mercy, have pity on me! You are called the refuge and hope of sinners; be my refuge and my hope. Help me, for the love of Jesus Christ; stretch forth your hand to a poor, fallen creature. I recommend myself to you, and I want to devote myself to your service forever. I bless and thank almighty God, who in his mercy has given me this confidence in you, that I hold to be a pledge of my eternal salvation. Mary, help me. Mother of Perpetual Help, never allow me to lose my God.

Pray three sequences of the Our Father, Hail Mary, and Glory Be.

June 29 » Saints Peter and Paul

Other Prayers and Observances in June

JULY

July 1 » Saint Junípero Serra

July 5 » Saint Elizabeth of Portugal

July 11 » Saint Benedict, Abbot

July 14 » Saint Kateri Tekakwitha

Kateri, favored child of God and Lily of the Mohawks, I come to seek your intercession in my present need: *[mention your intention]*. I admire the virtues that adorned your soul: love of God and neighbor, humility, obedience, patience, purity, and the spirit of sacrifice.

Help me to imitate your example in my state of life. Through the goodness and mercy of God, who has blessed you with so many graces that led you to the true faith and to a high degree of holiness, pray to God for me and help me.

Obtain for me a very fervent devotion to the Holy Eucharist so that I may love Holy Mass as you did and receive Holy Communion as often as I can. Teach me also to be devoted to my crucified Savior as you were, that I may cheerfully bear my daily crosses for love of him who suffered so much for love of me.

Most of all I beg you to pray for me that I may avoid sin, lead a holy life, and save my soul. Amen.

Recite three sets of the Our Faith, Hail Mary, and Glory.

Saint Kateri, Lily of the Mohawks, pray for me.

July 15 » Saint Bonaventure

July 16 » Our Lady of Mount Carmel

This novena is usually offered July 7-15 in preparation for the July 16 feast of Our Lady of Mount Carmel, but it can be prayed any time during the year. A three-day version of the novena uses only the prayer for the first day. (See page 93 to learn more about the Brown Scapular.)

At the end of each day, pause and mention your petitions. Recite the Our Father, Hail Mary, and Glory Be, and conclude:

Our Lady of Mount Carmel, pray for us.

First Day: O Beautiful Flower of Carmel, most fruitful vine, splendor of heaven, holy and singular, who brought forth the Son of God, still ever remaining a pure virgin, assist us in our necessity. O Star of the Sea, help and protect us. Show us that you are our Mother.

Second Day: Most Holy Mary, Our Mother, in your great love for us you gave us the Holy Scapular of Mount Carmel, having heard the prayers of your chosen son Saint Simon Stock. Help us now to wear it faithfully and with devotion.

May it be a sign to us of our desire to grow in holiness.

Third Day: O Queen of Heaven, you gave us the Scapular as an outward sign by which we might be known as your faithful children. May we always wear it with honor by avoiding sin and imitating your virtues. Help us to be faithful to this desire of ours.

Fourth Day: When you gave us, Gracious Lady, the Scapular as our habit, you called us to be not only servants, but also your own children. We ask you to gain for us from your Son the grace to live as your children in joy, peace, and love.

Fifth Day: O Mother of Fair Love, through your goodness, as your children we are called to live in the spirit of Carmel. Help us to live in charity with one another, prayerful as Elijah of old and mindful of our call to minister to God's people.

Sixth Day: With loving provident care, O Mother Most Amiable, you covered us with your Scapular as a shield of defense against the Evil One. Through your assistance, may we bravely struggle against the powers of evil, always open to your Son, Jesus Christ.

Seventh Day: O Mary, Help of Christians, you assured us that wearing your Scapular worthily would keep us safe from harm. Protect us in both body and soul with your continual aid. May all that we do be pleasing to your Son and to you.

Eighth Day: You give us hope, O Mother of Mercy, that through your Scapular promise we might quickly pass through the fires of purgatory to the Kingdom of your Son.

Be our comfort and our hope. Grant that our hope may not be in vain but that, ever faithful to your Son and to you, we may speedily enjoy after death the blessed company of Jesus and the saints.

Ninth Day: Most Holy Mother of Mount Carmel, when asked by a saint to grant privileges to the family of Carmel, you gave assurance of your motherly love and help to those faithful to you and to your Son. Behold us, your children. We glory in wearing your holy habit, that makes us members of your family of Carmel, through which we shall have your powerful protection in life, at death, and even after death. Look down with love, O Gate of Heaven, on all those now in their last agony. Look down graciously, O Virgin, Flower of Carmel, on all those in need of help. Look down mercifully, O Mother of our Savior, on all those who do not know that they are numbered among your children. Look down tenderly, O Queen of All Saints, on the poor souls.

....

July 18 » Saint Camillus de Lellis

July 22 » Saint Mary Magdalene

July 25 » Saint James

July 26 » Saints Joachim and Anne

This novena to Saint Anne, mother of the Blessed Virgin Mary, begins on July 17 and ends on the eve of the feast.

O glorious Saint Anne, filled with compassion for those who invoke you and with love for those who suffer, heavily laden with the weight of my troubles I cast myself at your feet and humbly beg of you to take under your special protection the present affair that I commend to you. *[Mention your intentions.]*

Be pleased to commend it to your daughter, the Blessed Virgin Mary, and lay it before the throne of Jesus, so that he may bring it to a happy outcome. Cease not to intercede for me until my request is granted. Above all, obtain for me the grace of one day beholding my God face to face and, with you and Mary and all the saints, of praising and blessing him for all eternity. Amen.

Good Saint Anne, mother of her who is our life, our sweetness, and our hope, pray to her for us and obtain our request.

Good Saint Anne, mother of her who is our life, our sweetness, and our hope, pray to her for us and obtain our request.

Good Saint Anne, mother of her who is our life, our sweetness, and our hope, pray to her for us and obtain our request.

Good Saint Anne, pray for us. Jesus, Mary, Anne.

July 29 » Saint Martha

Other Prayers and Observances in July

AUGUST

August 1 » Saint Alphonsus Liguori

....

August 4 » Saint John Vianney

The novena to this patron saint of parish priests begins on July 27.

I love you, O my God, and my only desire is to love you until the last breath of my life.

I love you, O my infinitely lovable God, and I would rather die loving you than live without loving you.

I love you, Lord, and the only grace I ask is to love you eternally.

My God, if my tongue cannot say in every moment that I love you, I want my heart to repeat it to you as often as I draw breath.

....

August 11 » Saint Philomena

While the feast of Saint Philomena is no longer on the liturgical calendar, her novena is prayed nine days before her former feast day or any time during the year.

O Faithful Virgin and glorious martyr, Saint Philomena, who works so many miracles on behalf of the poor and sorrowing, have pity on me. You know the multitude and diversity of my needs. Behold me at your feet, full of misery, but full of hope. I entreat your charity, O great Saint! Graciously hear me and obtain from God a favorable answer to the request I now humbly lay before thee. *[Mention your intention.]*

I am firmly convinced that through your merits, through the scorn, the sufferings, and the death you did endure, united to the merits of the Passion and death of Jesus, your Spouse, I shall obtain what I ask of you and, in the joy of my heart, I will bless God, who is admirable in his saints. Amen.

Saint Philomena, powerful with God, pray for us.
Saint Philomena, powerful with God, hear our prayers.

August 6 » The Transfiguration of the Lord

August 8 » Saint Dominic

August 10 » Saint Lawrence

August 11 » Saint Clare

August 15 » The Assumption of the Blessed Virgin Mary

O almighty and eternal God, you assumed into heaven, body and soul, the Immaculate Virgin Mary, Mother of your Son. Grant, through her intercession, that we may ever long for you and one day be brought to the glory of the resurrection. We ask this through Christ our Lord. Amen.

Pray the Our Father, Hail Mary, and Glory Be.

Queen, assumed into heaven, pray for us.

August 20 » Saint Bernard

August 22 » The Queenship of the Blessed Virgin Mary

August 24 » Saint Bartholomew

August 28 » Saint Augustine of Hippo

August 29 » The Passion of John the Baptist

Other Prayers and Observances in August

SEPTEMBER

September 3 » Saint Gregory the Great

September 8 » Nativity of the Blessed Virgin Mary

September 9 » Saint Peter Claver

September 12 » The Most Holy Name of Mary

September 13 » Saint John Chrysostom

September 14 » The Exaltation of the Holy Cross

....

September 15 » Our Lady of Sorrows
This novena begins on September 7.

Holy Mother of God, hear the prayers of the Church for all mothers, especially those wearied by life and overcome by the suffering they bear for their children.

Pray the Hail Mary and Glory Be.

O Mother of the Word Incarnate, intercede for them from your place in heaven, that the mercy of your divine Son might lighten their burden and give them strength.

Pray the Hail Mary and Glory Be.

As we contemplate this Mother, whose heart a sword has pierced, our thoughts go to all the suffering women in the world, suffering either physically or morally. In this suffering a woman's sensitivity plays a role, even though she often succeeds in resisting suffering better than a man. It is difficult to enumerate these sufferings; it is difficult to call them all by name. We may recall her maternal care for her children, especially when they fall sick or fall into bad ways; the death of those most dear to her; the loneliness of mothers forgotten by their grown-up children; the loneliness of widows; the sufferings of women who struggle alone to make a living; and the sufferings of women who have been wronged or exploited. Then there are the sufferings of conscience as a result of sin that has wounded the woman's human or maternal dignity, wounds of conscience that do not heal easily. With these sufferings too we must place ourselves at the foot of the Cross. (Mulieres Dignitatem, Saint John Paul II)

Recite the Hail Mary, the following prayer, the prayer for each day, and the Memorare after each day's prayer.

Prayer to Our Sorrowful Mother for a Particular Grace

O most holy and afflicted Virgin, Queen of Martyrs, who stood on Mount Calvary when your Son was in agony: by the sword of sorrow that pierced your heart, by the sufferings of your whole life on earth, by your unspeakable joy in Heaven, look down with maternal pity and tenderness as I kneel before you to sympathize with your sorrows and to place my petition, with childlike confidence, in your wounded heart.

I beg of you, dear Mother, to plead for me with your divine Son, since he can refuse you nothing and, through the merits of his most sacred Passion and Death together with your own suffering at the foot of his Cross, so to move his Sacred Heart that I may obtain this request *[mention your intention]*.

To whom shall I go in my need and misery, if not to you, O Mother most merciful, you who pity us poor exiles still sighing in this valley of tears? Offer to Jesus for us but one drop of his most precious blood, but one pang of his loving heart; remind him that you are our life, our sweetness, and our hope, and your prayer on my behalf will be heard. Amen.

First Day: Most sorrowful Virgin, sorrow filled your heart when, on offering your divine Son in the temple, holy Simeon told you that a sword would pierce your soul and you knew then that you would be asked to suffer with Jesus. I wish to join with you in this sorrow, and I ask you, O Queen of Martyrs, to obtain for me the grace that I may always remember my death, which will help to keep me from all sin.

Second Day: Most holy and sorrowful Virgin, sorrow filled your motherly heart when you saw your divine Son hated by Herod and you had to flee with him to Egypt to save him. I wish to join with you in this sorrow and ask you, O Queen of Martyrs, to obtain for me the grace to avoid all the temptations of my enemies on the difficult road to heaven.

Third Day: Most sorrowful Virgin, sorrow filled your heart when you were separated from your divine Son, who remained lost for three days in Jerusalem while you looked everywhere for him. I wish to join with you in the sorrow you felt then, and I ask you, O Queen of Martyrs, to obtain for me the grace never to lose Jesus your Son but always to remain united to him by the help of his grace.

Fourth Day: Most sorrowful Mother, sorrow filled your motherly heart when you followed your dear Son to Calvary and saw him falling under the weight of the Cross. I wish to join with you in this sorrow, and I ask you, O Queen of Martyrs, to obtain for me the grace to bear with patience whatever cross it will please God to send me.

Fifth Day: Most sorrowful Mother, the greatest sorrow filled your heart when you stood near the Cross of Jesus and watched him die in suffering for the sins of the world, without being able to do anything to help him. I wish to join with you in this sorrow, and I ask you, O Queen of Martyrs, to obtain for me the grace to fight against all my temptations, even though it costs me effort and suffering and death, so that, strengthened by his love when I am dying, I may obtain the grace of a happy death.

Sixth Day: Most Sorrowful Mother, sorrow filled your heart when the adorable body of your divine Son was taken down from the Cross and laid in your arms. I wish to join with you in this sorrow, and I ask you to obtain for me the grace to receive Jesus into my soul before I die, so that I may be perfectly united to him forever in heaven.

Seventh Day: Most sorrowful Virgin, sorrow again filled your heart when the sacred body of Jesus was taken from your arms and placed in the grave. I wish to join with you in this last sorrow of yours, and I ask you to obtain for me, through the sufferings of Jesus, that were the cause of all your sorrow, a sincere sorrow for my sins, a burning love for God, and a tender and practical devotion towards you.

Eighth Day

Pray the three novena prayers on pages 159.

Ninth Day

Pray the three novena prayers on pages 159.

September 16 » Saints Cornelius and Cyprian

September 20 » Saints Andrew Kim Tae-gŏn and Paul Chŏng Ha-Sang of Korea, and Companions

September 21 » Saint Matthew

September 23 » Saint Pius of Pietrelcina

September 27 » Saint Vincent de Paul

September 29 » Saints Michael, Gabriel, and Raphael

September 30 » Saint Jerome

Other Prayers and Observances in September

OCTOBER

October 1 » Saint Thérèse of the Child Jesus

O Little Thérèse of the Child Jesus, please pick for me a rose from the heavenly garden and send it to me as a message of love.

O Little Flower of Jesus, ask God to grant the favors I now place with confidence in your hands *[mention your special prayer request]*.

Saint Thérèse, help me to always believe as you did, in God's great love for me, so that I may imitate your "Little Way" each day.

October 4 » Saint Francis of Assisi

Lord, make me an instrument of your peace.
Where there is hatred, let me sow love;
where there is injury, pardon;
where there is doubt, faith;
where there is despair, hope;
where there is darkness, light;
and where there is sadness, joy.

O Divine Master, grant that I may not so much seek
to be consoled as to console;
to be understood as to understand;
to be loved as to love.

For it is in giving that we receive;
it is in pardoning that we are pardoned;
and it is in dying that we are born to eternal life. Amen.

October 5 » Blessed Francis Xavier Seelos

October 6 » Blessed Marie-Rose Durocher

October 7 » Our Lady of the Rosary

This novena begins on September 27 and includes the daily recitation of the Rosary.

My dearest Mother Mary, behold me, your child, in prayer at your feet. Accept this holy Rosary, that I offer you in accordance with your requests at Fatima, as a proof of my tender love for you, for the intentions of the Sacred Heart of Jesus, in atonement for the offenses committed against your Immaculate Heart, and for this special favor, that I earnestly request: *[mention your request]*.

I beg you to present my petition to your Divine Son. If you will pray for me, I cannot be refused. I know, dearest Mother, that you want me to seek God's holy will concerning my request. If what I ask for should not be granted, pray that I may receive that which will be of greater benefit to my soul.

I offer you a spiritual "Bouquet of Roses" because I love you. I put all my confidence in you, since your prayers before God are most powerful. For the greater glory of God and for the sake of Jesus, your loving Son, hear and grant my prayer. Sweet Heart of Mary, be my salvation.

....

October 11 » Saint John XXIII

October 15 » Saint Teresa of Jesus (Avila)

October 17 » Saint Ignatius of Antioch

October 18 » Saint Luke

October 19 » Saints John de Brébeuf, Isaac Jogues, and Companions

October 20 » Saint Paul of the Cross

October 22 » Saint John Paul II

October 28 » Saints Simon and Jude

Other Prayers and Observances in October

NOVEMBER

November 1 » All Saints

Litany of the Saints

Lord, have mercy.
Christ, have mercy.
Lord, have mercy.

Respond with "Pray for us" to each of the following invocations.

Holy Mary…
Michael, Gabriel, Raphael…
Angels of God…
Abraham, Moses, and Elijah…
Saint Joseph…
Saint John the Baptist…
Holy prophets…
Saint Peter and Saint Paul…
All holy apostles…
Saint Mary Magdalene…
All disciples of the Lord…
Saint Stephen…
Saint Perpetua and Saint Felicity…
Saint Agnes…
Saint Boniface…
Saint Thomas More…

Saint Charles Lwanga…
All holy martyrs…
Saint Augustine…
Saint Basil and Saint Gregory…
Saint John Chrysostom…
Saint Catherine…
Saint Martin…
Saint Patrick…
Saint Benedict…
Saint Francis…
Saint Clare…
Saint Francis Xavier…
Saint Vincent de Paul…
Saint Elizabeth…
Saint Therese…
Saint John Vianney…
All holy men and women…

Respond with "Lord, save your people" to each of the following.

Lord, be merciful…
From all harm…
From every sin…
From all temptations…
From everlasting death…

By your coming among us...
By your death and rising to new life...
By your gift of the Holy Spirit...

Respond with "Lord, hear our prayer" to each of the following.

Be merciful to us sinners...
Guide and protect your Holy Church...
Bring all peoples together in trust and peace...
Strengthen us in your service...
Jesus, Son of the living God...

Christ, hear us.
Lord Jesus, hear our prayer.

....

November 2 » All Souls

Jesus promised to be with those who call upon his name. Respond with "Be with us, Lord" to each of the following.

Trusting in his promise we say...
Sure and certain hope of your faithful dead...
Faithful friend in times of sorrow and doubt...
Voice that speaks peace to troubled hearts...
Beacon of light in moments of darkness...
Merciful Redeemer and fountain of forgiveness...
Enduring strength of all who mourn...

Gentle rest for your pilgrim people…

Pray the Our Father.

Lord God, whose days are without end and whose mercies beyond counting, keep us mindful that life is short and the hour of death unknown. Let your Spirit guide our days on earth in the ways of holiness and justice, that we may serve you in union with the whole Church, sure in faith, strong in hope, perfected in love. And when our earthly journey is ended, lead us rejoicing into your kingdom, where you live for ever and ever. Amen.

V. Eternal rest grant unto them, O Lord,
R. and let perpetual light shine upon them.

V. May they rest in peace.
R. Amen.

V. May their souls and the souls of all the faithful departed, through the mercy of God, rest in peace.
R. Amen.

November 4 » Saint Charles Borromeo

November 9 » The Dedication of the Lateran Basilica

November 10 » Saint Leo the Great

November 11 » Saint Martin of Tours

November 12 » Saint Josaphat

November 13 » Saint Frances Xavier Cabrini

November 17 » Saint Elizabeth of Hungary

November 18 » Saint Rose Philippine Duchesne

November 21 » The Presentation of the Blessed Virgin Mary

November 22 » Saint Cecilia

November 23 » Blessed Miguel Agustin Pro

November 24 » Saint Andrew Dũng-Lạc of Vietnam and Companions

---

November 30 » Saint Andrew

O glorious Saint Andrew, you were the first to recognize and follow the Lamb of God. With your friend Saint John you remained with Jesus for that first day, for your entire life, and now throughout eternity.

As you led your brother Saint Peter to Christ and many others after him, draw us also to him. Teach us to lead others to Christ solely out of love for him and dedication in his service. Help us to learn the lesson of the Cross and to carry our daily crosses without complaint so that they may carry us to Jesus. Amen.

Other Prayers and Observances in November

DECEMBER

December 3 » Saint Francis Xavier

The following is Saint Francis Xavier's prayer for unbelievers. See page 136 for the Novena of Grace in honor of this saint.

Eternal God, Creator of all things, remember that the souls of unbelievers have been created by you and formed to your own image and likeness. Behold, O Lord, how to your dishonor hell is being filled with these very souls. Remember that Jesus Christ, your Son, for their salvation suffered a most cruel death. Do not permit, O Lord, we beseech you, that your divine Son be any longer despised by unbelievers but rather, being appeased by the prayers of your saints and the Church, the most holy spouse of your Son, deign to be mindful of your mercy and, forgetting their idolatry and their unbelief, bring them to know him whom you did send, Jesus Christ, your Son, our Lord, who is our health, life, and resurrection and through whom we have been redeemed and saved and to whom be all glory forever. Amen.

Pray for us, Saint Francis Xavier, that we may be made worthy of the promises of Christ.

O God, who did deign, by the preaching and miracles of Saint Francis Xavier, to join unto your Church the nations of the Indies, grant, we beseech you, that we who reverence his glorious merits may also imitate his example, through Jesus Christ our Lord. Amen.

December 7 » Saint Ambrose of Milan

December 8 » The Immaculate Conception
of the Blessed Virgin Mary

This novena begins on November 29, but it can be prayed any time during the year.

Immaculate Virgin Mary, you were pleasing in the sight of God from the first moment of your conception in the womb of your mother, Saint Anne. You were chosen to be the mother of Jesus Christ, the Son of God. I believe the teaching of the Church that in the first instant of your conception, by the singular grace and privilege of Almighty God, in virtue of the merits of Jesus Christ, Savior of the human race and your beloved Son, you were preserved from all stain of original sin. I thank God for this wonderful privilege and grace bestowed upon you as I honor your Immaculate Conception.

Look graciously upon me as I implore this special favor: *[mention your request].*

Virgin Immaculate, Mother of God and my Mother, from your throne in heaven turn your eyes of pity upon me. Filled with confidence in your goodness and power, I beg you to help me in this journey of life, which is so full of dangers for my soul. I entrust myself entirely to you that I may never be the slave of the devil through sin but may always live a humble and pure life. I consecrate myself to you forever, for my only desire is to love your divine Son, Jesus. Mary, since none of your devout servants has perished, may I too be saved. Amen.

Litany of the Blessed Virgin Mary

Lord, have mercy on us.

Christ, have mercy on us.

Lord, have mercy on us.

Christ, hear us.

Christ, graciously hear us.

God the Father of Heaven, have mercy on us.

God the Son, Redeemer of the world, have mercy on us.

God the Holy Spirit, have mercy on us.

Holy Trinity, one God, have mercy on us.

Respond with "Pray for us" to each of the following invocations.

Holy Mary…

Holy Mother of God…

Holy Virgin of virgins…

Mother of divine grace…

Mother most pure…

Mother most chaste…

Mother inviolate…

Mother undefiled…

Mother most amiable…

Mother most admirable...
Mother of good counsel...
Mother of our Creator...
Mother of our Savior...
Virgin most prudent...
Virgin most venerable...
Virgin most renowned...
Virgin most powerful...
Virgin most merciful...
Virgin most faithful...
Mirror of justice...
Seat of wisdom...
Cause of our joy...
Spiritual vessel...
Vessel of honor...
Singular vessel of devotion...
Mystical rose...
Tower of David...
Tower of ivory...
House of gold...
Ark of the Covenant,...
Gate of Heaven...
Morning star...
Health of the sick...

Refuge of sinners...
Comforter of the afflicted...
Help of Christians...
Queen of angels...
Queen of patriarchs...
Queen of prophets...
Queen of apostles...
Queen of martyrs...
Queen of confessors...
Queen of virgins...
Queen of all saints...
Queen conceived without Original Sin...
Queen assumed into Heaven...
Queen of the most holy Rosary...
Queen of peace...

Lamb of God, who takes away the sins of the world, spare us, O Lord.

Lamb of God, who takes away the sins of the world, graciously hear us, O Lord.

Lamb of God, who takes away the sins of the world, have mercy on us.

Pray for us, O Holy Mother of God, that we may be made worthy of the promises of Christ.

Grant, we beseech you, O Lord God, that we your servants may enjoy perpetual health of mind and body and by the glorious intercession of the Blessed Mary, ever Virgin, be delivered from present sorrow and enjoy eternal happiness. Through Christ our Lord. Amen.

The following prayer is recited on the feast day.

Father, you prepared the Virgin Mary to be the worthy mother of your Son. You let her share beforehand in the salvation Christ would bring by his death, and you kept her sinless from the first moment of her conception. Help us by her prayers to live in your presence without sin. We ask this through our Lord Jesus Christ, your Son, who lives and reigns with you and the Holy Spirit, one God, forever and ever. Amen.

December 9 » Saint Juan Diego of Mexico

December 12 » Our Lady of Guadalupe

This novena begins on December 4. Each day's prayer is followed by the Our Father, Hail Mary, Glory Be, and the following Memorare of Our Lady of Guadalupe.

Remember, O most gracious Virgin of Guadalupe, that in your heavenly apparitions on the mount of Tepeyac, you promised to show your compassion and pity towards all who, loving and trusting you, seek your help and call upon you in their necessities and afflictions. You promised to hear our supplications, to dry our tears, and to give us consolation and relief.

Never has it been known that anyone who fled to your protection, implored your help, or sought your intercession, was left unaided. Inspired by this confidence, we fly to you, O Mary, Ever-Virgin Mother of the true God! Though grieving under the weight of our sins, we come to prostrate ourselves before you. We fully trust that, standing beneath your shadow and protection, nothing will trouble or afflict us, nor do we need to fear illness or misfortune or any other sorrow.

O Virgin of Guadalupe, you want to remain with us through your admirable image, you who are our Mother, our health, and our life. Placing ourselves beneath your maternal gaze and having recourse to you in all our necessities, we need do nothing more.

O Holy Mother of God, despise not our petitions, but in your mercy hear and answer us. Amen.

First Day: Dearest Lady of Guadalupe, fruitful Mother of holiness, teach me your ways of gentleness and strength. Hear my humble prayer offered with heartfelt confidence to beg this favor *[mention your intention]*.

Second Day: Mary, conceived without sin, I come to your throne of grace to share the fervent devotion of your faithful Mexican children who call to you under the glorious Aztec title of "Guadalupe." Obtain for me a lively faith to do your Son's holy will always. May his will be done on earth as it is in heaven.

Third Day: Mary, whose Immaculate Heart was pierced by seven swords of grief, help me to walk valiantly amid the sharp thorns strewn across my pathway. Obtain for me the strength to be a true imitator of you. This I ask you, my dear Mother.

Fourth Day: Dearest Mother of Guadalupe, I beg you for a fortified will to imitate your divine Son's charity, to always seek the good of others in need. Grant me this, I humbly ask of you.

Fifth Day: Most Holy Mother, I beg you to obtain for me pardon of all my sins, abundant graces to serve your Son more faithfully from now on, and the grace to praise him with you forever in heaven.

Sixth Day: Mary, Mother of vocations, multiply priestly vocations and fill the earth with religious houses that will be light and warmth for the world, safety in stormy nights. Beg your Son to send us many priests and religious. This we ask of you, O Mother.

Seventh Day: Lady of Guadalupe, we beg you that parents live a holy life and educate their children in a Christian manner, that children obey and follow the directions of their parents, and that all members of the family pray and worship together. This we ask of you, O Mother.

Eighth Day: With my heart full of the most sincere veneration, I prostrate myself before you, O Mother, to ask you to obtain for me the grace to fulfill the duties of my state in life with faithfulness and constancy.

Ninth Day: God, you have been pleased to bestow upon us unceasing favors by having placed us under the special protection of the Most Blessed Virgin Mary. Grant us, your humble servants, who rejoice in honoring her today upon earth, the happiness of seeing her face-to-face in heaven.

December 13 » Saint Lucy of Syracuse

December 14 » Saint John of the Cross

December 25 » The Nativity of the Lord (Christmas)

This Christmas novena begins on December 16.

Divine Infant, after the wonders of your birth in Bethlehem, you wished to extend your infinite mercy to the whole world by calling the Wise Men through heavenly inspiration to your crib, which was in this way changed into a royal throne. You graciously received those holy men, who were obedient to the divine call and hastened to your feet. They recognized and worshipped you as Prince of Peace, the Redeemer of humankind, and the very Son of God.

Show us also your goodness and almighty power. Enlighten our minds, strengthen our wills, and inflame our hearts to know you, to serve you, and to love you in this life, that we may merit to find our joy in you eternally in the life to come.

O Jesus, most powerful Child, I implore you again to help me: *[mention your request]*.

Divine Child, great omnipotent God, I implore through your most Holy Mother's most powerful intercession, and through the boundless mercy of your omnipotence as God, for a favorable answer to my prayer during this novena.

Grant me the grace of possessing you eternally with Mary and Joseph and of adoring you with your holy angels and saints. Amen.

December 26 » Saint Stephen

December 27 » Saint John

O glorious Saint John, you were so loved by Jesus that you merited to rest your head upon his breast and to be left in his place as a son to Mary. Obtain for us an ardent love for Jesus and Mary. Let me be united with them now on earth and forever after in heaven. Amen.

December 28 » The Holy Innocents

December 31 »Vigil of the Solemnity of Mary, Mother of God
Te Deum

O God, we praise you and acknowledge you to be the supreme Lord. Everlasting Father, all the earth worships you. All the Angels, the heavens, all angelic powers, all the Cherubim and Seraphim continuously cry to you:

> Holy, Holy, Holy, Lord God of Hosts!
> Heaven and earth are full of the majesty of your glory.

The glorious choir of the Apostles, the wonderful company of Prophets, the white-robed army of Martyrs, praise you. The holy Church throughout the world acknowledges you: the Father of Infinite Majesty; your adorable, true and only Son; and the Holy Spirit, the Comforter.

O Christ, you are the King of glory! You are the everlasting Son of the Father. When you took it upon yourself to deliver humankind, you did not disdain the Virgin's womb. Having overcome the sting of death, you opened the Kingdom of Heaven to all believers. You sit at the right hand of God in the glory of the Father. We believe that you will come to be our Judge. We, therefore, beg you to help your servants, whom you have redeemed with your Precious Blood. Let us be numbered with your saints in everlasting glory.

V. Save your people, O Lord, and bless your inheritance!
R. Govern them, and raise them up forever.

V. Every day we thank you.
R. And we praise your Name forever, yes, forever and ever.

V. O Lord, deign to keep us from sin this day.
R. Have mercy on us, O Lord, have mercy on us.

V. Let your mercy, O Lord, be upon us,
for we have hoped in you.
R. O Lord, in you I have put my trust;
let me never be put to shame.

Other Prayers and Observances in December

LENT AND PASSIONTIDE

Recite this short prayer every Friday.

Behold, O good and sweetest Jesus.

....

EASTER NOVENA

Begin this novena nine days before Easter, praying the following each day.

Jesus, I believe that by your own power you rose from death, as you promised, a glorious victor. May this mystery strengthen my hope in another and better life after death, the resurrection of my body on the last day, and an eternity of happiness.

I firmly hope that you will keep your promise to me and raise me up glorified. Through your glorious Resurrection, I hope you will make my body like your own in glory and life and permit me to dwell with you in heaven for all eternity.

I believe that your Resurrection is the crown of your life and work as God-Man, because it is your glorification. This is the beginning of the glorious life that was due to you as the Son of God. Your Resurrection is also the reward of your life of suffering.

Jesus, my Risen Lord and King, I adore your sacred humanity, which received this eternal Kingdom of honor, power, joy, and glory. I rejoice with you, my Master, glorious, immortal, and all-powerful.

Through the glorious mystery of your Resurrection, I ask you to help me to rise with you spiritually and to live a life free from sin, that I may be bent upon doing God's will in all things and be patient in suffering. Through the sacraments, may my soul be enriched evermore with sanctifying grace, the source of Divine life. I also ask that you grant me this special request: *[mention your request]*. May your will be done!

DIVINE MERCY NOVENA

This feast is celebrated on the Sunday after Easter. Begin the Novena of Chaplets to the Divine Mercy on Good Friday. Start each day's prayer with the Our Father, Hail Mary, and Creed. Following the prayer of the day, offer the Chaplet of Divine Mercy. See page 111.

Good Friday

> *Today bring to me ALL MANKIND, ESPECIALLY ALL SINNERS and immerse them in the ocean of my mercy. In this way you will console me in the bitter grief into which the loss of souls plunges me.*

Most Merciful Jesus, whose very nature it is to have compassion on us and to forgive us, do not look upon our sins but upon our trust, that we place in your infinite goodness. Receive us all into the abode of your Most Compassionate

Heart, and never let us escape from it. We beg this of you by your love that unites you to the Father and the Holy Spirit.

Eternal Father, turn your merciful gaze upon all humankind and especially upon poor sinners, all enfolded in the Most Compassionate Heart of Jesus. For the sake of his sorrowful Passion show us your mercy, that we may praise the omnipotence of your mercy for ever and ever. Amen.

Holy Saturday

Today bring to me THE SOULS OF PRIESTS AND RELIGIOUS and immerse them in my unfathomable mercy. It was they who gave me strength to endure my bitter Passion. Through them as through channels my mercy flows out upon humankind.

Most Merciful Jesus, from whom comes all that is good, increase your grace in men and women consecrated to your service that they may perform worthy works of mercy and that all who see them may glorify the Father of Mercy, who is in heaven.

Eternal Father, turn your merciful gaze upon the company of chosen ones in your vineyard — upon the souls of priests and religious — and endow them with the strength of your blessing. For the love of the heart of your Son in which they are enfolded, impart to them your power and light that they may be able to guide others in the way of salvation and with one voice sing praise to your boundless mercy for ages without end. Amen.

Easter Sunday

Today bring to me ALL DEVOUT AND FAITHFUL SOULS and immerse then in the ocean of my mercy. The souls brought me consolation on the Way of the Cross. They were that drop of consolation in the midst of an ocean of bitterness.

Most Merciful Jesus, from the treasury of your mercy, you impart your graces in great abundance to each and all. Receive us into the abode of your Most Compassionate Heart and never let us escape from it. We beg this grace of you by that most wondrous love for the heavenly Father with which your heart burns so fiercely.

Eternal Father, turn your merciful gaze upon faithful souls, as upon the inheritance of your Son. For the sake of his sorrowful Passion, grant them your blessing and surround them with your constant protection. Thus may they never fail in love or lose the treasure of the holy faith but rather, with all the hosts of angels and saints, may they glorify your boundless mercy for endless ages. Amen.

Monday within the Octave of Easter

Today bring to me THOSE WHO DO NOT BELIEVE IN GOD AND THOSE WHO DO NOT YET KNOW ME. I was thinking also of them during my bitter Passion, and their future zeal comforted my heart. Immerse them in the ocean of my mercy.

Most compassionate Jesus, you are the light of the whole world. Receive into the abode of your Most Compassionate

Heart the souls of those who do not believe in God and of those who as yet do not know you. Let the rays of your grace enlighten them so that they, too, together with us, may extol your wonderful mercy; and do not let them escape from the abode that is your Most Compassionate Heart.

Eternal Father, turn your merciful gaze upon the souls of those who do not believe in you and of those who as yet do not know you but are enclosed in the Most Compassionate Heart of Jesus. Draw them to the light of the Gospel. These souls do not know what great happiness it is to love you. Grant that they, too, may extol the generosity of your mercy for endless ages. Amen.

Tuesday within the Octave of Easter

> *Today bring to me THE SOULS OF THOSE WHO HAVE SEPARATED THEMSELVES FROM MY CHURCH and immerse them in the ocean of my mercy. During my bitter Passion they tore at my body and heart, that is, my Church. As they return to unity with the Church, my wounds heal and in this way they alleviate my Passion.*

Most Merciful Jesus, you are goodness itself. Do not refuse light to those who seek it of you. Receive into the abode of your Most Compassionate Heart the souls of those who have separated themselves from your Church. Draw them by your light into the unity of the Church, and do not let them escape from the abode of your Most Compassionate Heart; but bring it about that they, too, come to glorify the generosity of your mercy.

Eternal Father, turn your merciful gaze upon the souls of those who have separated themselves from your Son's Church, who have squandered your blessings and misused your graces by obstinately persisting in their errors. Do not look upon their errors but upon the love of your own Son and upon his bitter Passion, that he underwent for their sake since they, too, are enclosed in his Most Compassionate Heart. Bring it about that they also may glorify your great mercy for endless ages. Amen.

Wednesday within the Octave of Easter

> *Today bring to me THE MEEK AND HUMBLE SOULS AND THE SOULS OF LITTLE CHILDREN and immerse them in my mercy. These souls most closely resemble my heart. They strengthened me during my bitter agony. I saw them as earthly angels who will keep vigil at my altars. I pour out upon them whole torrents of grace. Only the humble soul is capable of receiving my grace. I favor humble souls with my confidence.*

Most Merciful Jesus, you yourself have said, "Learn from me for I am meek and humble of heart." Receive into the abode of your Most Compassionate Heart all meek and humble souls and the souls of little children. These souls send all heaven into ecstasy and they are the heavenly Father's favorites. They are a sweet-smelling bouquet before the throne of God; God himself takes delight in their fragrance. These souls have a permanent abode in your Most Compassionate Heart, O Jesus, and they unceasingly sing out a hymn of love and mercy.

Eternal Father, turn your merciful gaze upon meek souls, upon humble souls, and upon little children who are enfolded in the abode which is the Most Compassionate Heart of Jesus. These souls bear the closest resemblance to your Son. Their fragrance rises from the earth and reaches your very throne. Father of mercy and of all goodness, I beg you by the love you bear these souls and by the delight you take in them: Bless the whole world, that all souls together may sing out the praises of your mercy for endless ages. Amen.

Thursday within the Octave of Easter

> *Today bring to me THE SOULS WHO ESPECIALLY VENERATE AND GLORIFY MY MERCY and immerse them in my mercy. These souls sorrowed most over my Passion and entered most deeply into my spirit. They are living images of my Compassionate Heart. These souls will shine with a special brightness in the next life. Not one of them will go into the fire of hell. I shall particularly defend each one of them at the hour of death.*

Most Merciful Jesus, whose heart is love itself, receive into the abode of your Most Compassionate Heart the souls of those who particularly extol and venerate the greatness of your mercy. These souls are mighty with the very power of God himself. In the midst of all afflictions and adversities they go forward, confident of your mercy and, united to you, O Jesus, they carry all humankind on their shoulders. These souls will not be judged severely, but your mercy will embrace them as they depart from this life.

Eternal Father, turn your merciful gaze upon the souls who glorify and venerate your greatest attribute, that of your fathomless mercy, and who are enclosed in the Most Compassionate Heart of Jesus. These souls are a living Gospel; their hands are full of deeds of mercy and their hearts, overflowing with joy, sing a canticle of mercy to you, O Most High! I beg you, O God:

Show them your mercy according to the hope and trust they have placed in you. Let there be accomplished in them the promise of Jesus that during their life, but especially at the hour of death, the souls who will venerate his fathomless mercy he himself will defend as his glory. Amen.

Friday within the Octave of Easter

> *Today bring to me THE SOULS WHO ARE DETAINED IN PURGATORY and immerse them in the abyss of my mercy. Let the torrents of my blood cool down their scorching flames. All these souls are greatly loved by me. They are making retribution to my justice. It is in your power to bring them relief. Draw all the indulgences from the treasury of my Church and offer them on their behalf. Oh, if you only knew the torments they suffer you would continually offer for them the alms of the spirit and pay off their debt to my justice.*

Most Merciful Jesus, you yourself have said that you desire mercy; so I bring into the abode of your Most Compassionate Heart the souls in Purgatory, souls who are very dear to you and yet must make retribution to your justice. May the streams of blood and water that gushed forth from your heart put out the flames of Purgatory that there, too, the power of your mercy may be celebrated.

Eternal Father, turn your merciful gaze upon the souls suffering in Purgatory, who are enfolded in the Most Compassionate Heart of Jesus. I beg you, by the sorrowful Passion of Jesus, your Son, and by all the bitterness with which his most sacred soul was flooded: Manifest your mercy to the souls who are under your just scrutiny. Look upon them in no other way but only through the wounds of Jesus, your dearly beloved Son; for we firmly believe that there is no limit to your goodness and compassion. Amen.

Saturday within the Octave of Easter

> *Today bring to me SOULS WHO HAVE BECOME LUKEWARM and immerse them in the abyss of my mercy. These souls wound my heart most painfully. My soul suffered the most dreadful loathing in the Garden of Olives because of lukewarm souls. They were the reason I cried out: "Father, take this cup away from me, if it be your will." For them, the last hope of salvation is to run to my mercy.*

Most compassionate Jesus, you are compassion itself. I bring lukewarm souls into the abode of your Most Compassionate Heart. In this fire of your pure love, let these tepid souls, who, like corpses, filled you with such deep loathing, be once again set aflame. O Most Compassionate Jesus, exercise the omnipotence of your mercy and draw them into the very ardor of your love and bestow upon them the gift of holy love, for nothing is beyond your power.

Eternal Father, turn your merciful gaze upon lukewarm souls who are nonetheless enfolded in the Most Compassionate Heart of Jesus. Father of Mercy, I beg you by the bitter Passion of your Son and by his three-hour agony on the Cross: Let them, too, glorify the abyss of your mercy. Amen.

ASCENSION

Begin this novena nine days before the Feast of the Ascension.

Jesus, I honor you on the feast of your Ascension into heaven. I rejoice with all my heart at the glory into which you entered to reign as King of Heaven and Earth. When the struggle of this life is over, give me the grace to share your joy and triumph in heaven for all eternity.

I believe that you entered into your glorious Kingdom to prepare a place for me, for you promised to come again to take me to yourself. Grant that I may seek only the joys of your friendship and love, so that I may deserve to be united with you in heaven.

In the hour of my own homecoming, when I appear before your Father to give an account of my life on earth, have mercy on me.

Jesus, in your love for me you have brought me from evil to good and from misery to happiness. Give me the grace to rise above my human weakness. May your humanity give me courage in my weakness and free me from my sins.

Through your grace give me the courage of perseverance for you have called and justified me by faith. May I hold fast to the life you have given me and come to the eternal gifts you promised.

You love me, dear Jesus. Help me to love you in return. I ask you to grant this special favor: *[mention your request].*

By your unceasing care, guide my steps toward the life of glory you have prepared for those who love you. Help me grow in holiness and thank you by my life of faithful service.

....

PENTECOST

Begin this novena nine days before Pentecost. At the conclusion of each day's prayer, say one Our Father, one Hail Mary, seven Glory Be's, and the following Act of Consecration and Prayer for the Seven Gifts.

Act of Consecration to the Holy Spirit

On my knees before the great multitude of heavenly witnesses, I offer myself, soul and body to you, Eternal Spirit of God. I adore the brightness of your purity, the unerring keenness of your justice, and the might of your love. You are the strength and light of my soul. In you I live and move and am. I desire never to grieve you by unfaithfulness to grace and I pray with all my heart to be kept from the smallest sin against you. Mercifully guard my every thought and grant that I may always watch for your light, and listen to your voice, and follow your gracious inspirations. I cling to you and give myself to you and ask you, by your compassion, to watch over me in my weakness. Holding the pierced feet of Jesus and looking at his five wounds, and trusting in his precious blood and adoring his opened side and stricken heart, I implore you, Adorable Spirit, helper of my infirmity, to keep me in your grace that I may never sin against you. Give me grace O Holy Spirit, Spirit of the Father and the Son, to say to you always and everywhere, "Speak Lord, for your servant is listening." Amen.

Prayer for the Seven Gifts of the Holy Spirit

O Lord Jesus Christ who, before ascending into heaven did promise to send the Holy Spirit to finish your work in the souls of your apostles and disciples, deign to grant the same Holy Spirit to me that he may perfect in my soul the work of your grace and your love. Grant me the Spirit of Wisdom that I may despise the perishable things of this world and aspire only after the things that are eternal; the Spirit of Understanding to enlighten my mind with the light of your divine truth; the Spirit on Counsel that I may ever choose the surest way of pleasing God and gaining heaven; the Spirit of Fortitude that I may bear my cross with you and overcome with courage all the obstacles that oppose my salvation; the Spirit of Knowledge that I may know God and know myself and grow perfect in the science of the saints; the Spirit of Piety that I may find the service of God sweet and amiable; and the Spirit of Awe that I may be filled with a loving reverence towards God and dread in any way to displease him. Mark me, dear Lord with the sign of your true disciples, and animate me in all things with your Spirit. Amen.

First Day: Almighty and eternal God, who have regenerated us by water and the Holy Spirit and given us forgiveness of all sins, vouchsafe to send forth from heaven upon us your sevenfold Spirit, the Spirit of Wisdom and Understanding, the Spirit of Counsel and Fortitude, the Spirit of Knowledge and Piety, and fill us with the Spirit of Awe. Amen.

Second Day: Come, O blessed Spirit of Awe, penetrate my inmost heart that I may set you, my Lord and God, before my face forever. Help me to shun all things that can offend you and make me worthy to appear before the pure eyes of your Divine Majesty in heaven, where you live and reign in the unity of the ever Blessed Trinity, God, world without end. Amen.

Third Day: Come, O Blessed Spirit of Piety, possess my heart. Enkindle therein such a love for God that I may find satisfaction only in divine service and for God's sake lovingly submit to all legitimate authority. Amen.

Fourth Day: Come, O Blessed Spirit of Fortitude, uphold my soul in time of trouble and adversity, sustain my efforts after holiness, strengthen my weakness, give me courage against all the assaults of my enemies that I may never be overcome and separated from you, my God and greatest good. Amen.

Fifth Day: Come, O Blessed Spirit of Knowledge, and grant that I may perceive the will of the Father; show me the nothingness of earthly things that I may realize their vanity and use them only for your glory and my own salvation, looking ever beyond them to you and your eternal rewards. Amen.

Sixth Day: Come, O Spirit of Understanding, and enlighten our minds that we may know and believe all the mysteries of salvation, merit at last to see the eternal light in your Divine light, and in the light of your glory have a clear vision of you and the Father and the Son. Amen.

Seventh Day: Come, O Spirit of Counsel, help and guide me in all my ways that I may always do your holy will. Incline my heart to that which is good, turn it away from all that is evil, and direct me by the straight path of your commandments to that goal of eternal life for which I long. Amen

Eighth Day: Come, O Spirit of Wisdom, and reveal to my soul the mysteries of heavenly things, their exceeding greatness, power, and beauty. Teach me to love them above and beyond all the passing joys and satisfactions of earth. Help me to attain them and possess them forever. Amen.

Ninth Day: Come, O Divine Spirit, fill my heart with your heavenly fruits, your charity, joy, peace, patience, benignity, goodness, faith, mildness, and temperance, that I may never weary in the service of God but by continued faithful submission to your inspiration may merit to be united eternally with you in the love of the Father and the Son. Amen.

TRINITY SUNDAY

Offer this prayer in praise of the Trinity.

With our whole heart and voice we glorify you, we praise you, we bless you, God the Father unbegotten, the only-begotten Son, the Holy Spirit, the Paraclete, the holy and undivided Trinity.

For you are great and do wonderful things: You alone are God. To you be praise, to you glory, to you thanksgiving forever and ever, O blessed Trinity!

CORPUS CHRISTI

Begin the Novena to the Sacred Heart of Jesus on this feast. See page 146 for a longer version.

O my Jesus, you have said: "Truly I say to you, ask and you will receive, seek and you will find, knock and it will be opened to you." Behold I knock, I seek, and I ask for the grace of *[name your request]*.

Pray an Our Father, Hail Mary, and Glory Be.

Sacred Heart of Jesus, I place all my trust in you.

ANY TIME OF THE YEAR

Novena to Saint Anthony for Any Need

Saint Anthony, you are glorious for your miracles and for the humble act of Jesus, who came as a little child to lie in your arms. Obtain for me from his bounty the grace I ardently desire. You were so compassionate toward sinners, do not regard my unworthiness. Let the glory of God be magnified by you in connection with the particular request that I earnestly present to you. *[State your request.]*

As a pledge of my gratitude, I promise to live more faithfully in accordance with the teachings of the Church and to be devoted to the service of the poor, whom you loved and still love so greatly. Bless this resolution of mine that I may be faithful to it until death.

Saint Anthony, consoler of all the afflicted, pray for me.

Saint Anthony, helper of all who invoke you, pray for me.

Saint Anthony, whom the Infant Jesus loved and honored so much, pray for me. Amen.

Other Prayers

ROSARY NOVENA TO OUR LADY

In an apparition of Our Lady of Pompeii, which occurred in 1884 at Naples, in the house of Commander Agrelli, the heavenly Mother deigned to make known the manner in which she desires to be invoked. For thirteen months Fortuna Agrelli, the daughter of the Commander, had endured dreadful sufferings and torturous cramps. The most celebrated physicians had given up. On February 16, 1884, the afflicted girl and her relatives commenced a novena of Rosaries. The Queen of the Holy Rosary favored her with an apparition on March 3. Mary, sitting upon a high throne, surrounded by luminous figures, held the divine Child on her lap, and in her hand a Rosary. They were accompanied by Saint Dominic and Saint Catherine of Siena. Mary looked upon the sufferer with maternal tenderness and the patient saluted her with the words: "Queen of the Holy Rosary, be gracious to me; restore me to health! I have already prayed to thee in a novena, O Mary, but have not yet experienced thy aid. I am so anxious to be cured!" "Child," responded the Blessed Virgin, "you have invoked me by various titles and have always obtained favors from me. Now, since you have called me by that title so pleasing to me, 'Queen of the Holy Rosary', I can no longer refuse the favor your petition; for this name is most precious and dear to me. Make three novenas, and you shall obtain all." Once more the Queen of the Holy Rosary appeared to her and said: "Whoever desires to obtain favors from me should make three novenas of the prayers of the Rosary, and three novenas in thanksgiving." This miracle of the Rosary made a very deep impression on Pope Leo XIII and greatly contributed to the fact that, in many circular letters, he urged all Christians to love the Rosary and say it fervently.

Method

The Rosary Novena to Our Lady consists of five decades of the Rosary prayed each day for twenty-seven days in petition, then immediately five decades prayed each day for twenty-seven days in thanksgiving, whether or not the request has been granted. The meditations vary from day to day, as on the following pages.

On the first day meditate on the Joyful Mysteries; on the second day the Luminous Mysteries; on the third day the Sorrowful Mysteries; and on the fourth day the Glorious Mysteries; and so on throughout the fifty-four days. Or you may pray the mysteries on the days of the week as outlined on pages 41-50.

This is an arduous novena but it is a novena of love. If you are sincere, you can trust that Our Lady will hear your request and intercede for you with God. Should you not obtain the favor you seek, be assured that the Queen of the Holy Rosary, who knows what each one of us needs most, has heard your prayer. You will not have prayed in vain. No prayer ever went unheard, and Our Blessed Lady has never been known to fail. Look upon each Hail Mary as a rare and beautiful rose that you lay at Mary's feet. These spiritual roses, bound in a wreath with Spiritual Communions, will be a most pleasing and acceptable gift to her and will bring down upon you special graces.

A novena record is provided on page 222.

THE JOYFUL MYSTERIES

In petition

Hail, Queen of the Most Holy Rosary, my Mother Mary, Hail! At your feet I humbly pray and offer to you a Crown of Roses — snow-white buds to remind you of your joys — each bud recalling to you a holy mystery; each ten bound together with my petition for a particular grace.

Or in thanksgiving

Hail, Queen of the Most Holy Rosary, my Mother Mary, hail! At your feet I gratefully pray and offer to you a crown of roses — snow-white buds to remind you of your joys — each bud recalling to you a holy mystery; each ten bound together with my petition for a particular grace.

Make the Sign of the Cross and pray the Creed, an Our Father, three Hail Marys, Glory Be, and Decade Prayer (see page 41).

I. The Annunciation

Sweet Mother Mary, meditating on the mystery of the Annunciation, when the angel Gabriel appeared to you with the tidings that you were to become the Mother of God; greeting you with that sublime salutation, "Hail, full of grace! The Lord is with thee!" and you did humbly submit yourself to the will of the Father, responding: "Behold the handmaid of the Lord. Be it done unto me according to thy word," I humbly pray:

Say an Our Father, ten Hail Marys, Glory Be, and Decade Prayer.

I bind these snow-white buds with a petition for the virtue of Humility and humbly lay this bouquet at your feet.

II. The Visitation

Sweet Mother Mary, meditating on the mystery of the Visitation, when, upon your visit to your cousin, Elizabeth, she greeted you with the prophetic utterance, "Blessed are you among women, and blessed is the fruit of your womb!" and you did answer with that Canticle of Canticles, the Magnificat, I humbly pray:

Say an Our Father, ten Hail Marys, Glory Be, and Decade Prayer.

I bind these snow-white buds with a petition for the virtue of Charity and humbly lay this bouquet at your feet.

III. The Nativity

Sweet Mother Mary, meditating on the mystery of the Nativity of our Lord, when, your time being completed, you did bring forth, O holy Virgin, the Redeemer of the world in a stable at Bethlehem; whereupon choirs of angels filled the heavens with their exultant song of praise — "Glory to God in the highest, and on earth peace to men of good will," I humbly pray:

Say an Our Father, ten Hail Marys, Glory Be, and Decade Prayer.

I bind these snow-white buds with a petition for the virtue of Detachment from the World and humbly lay this bouquet at your feet.

IV. The Presentation

Sweet Mother Mary, meditating on the mystery of the Presentation, when, in obedience to the Law of Moses, you did present the Child in the Temple, where the holy prophet Simeon, taking the Child in his arms, offered thanks to God for sparing him to look upon his Savior and foretold your sufferings by the words: "Your soul also a sword shall pierce," I humbly pray:

Say an Our Father, ten Hail Marys, Glory Be, and Decade Prayer.

I bind these snow-white buds with a petition for the virtue of Purity and humbly lay this bouquet at your feet.

V. The Finding of the Child Jesus in the Temple

Sweet Mother Mary, meditating on the mystery of the finding of the Child Jesus in the Temple, when having sought him for three days, sorrowing, your heart was gladdened upon finding him in the Temple speaking to the doctors; and when, upon your request, he obediently returned home with you, I humbly pray:

Say an Our Father, ten Hail Marys, Glory Be, and Decade Prayer.

I bind these snow-white buds with a petition for the virtue of Obedience to the will of God and humbly lay this bouquet at your feet.

For the concluding prayers go to page 221.

THE LUMINOUS MYSTERIES

In petition

Hail, Queen of the Most Holy Rosary, my Mother Mary, Hail! At your feet I humbly pray and offer to you a Crown of Roses — bright yellow roses to remind thee of thy ministry of your son — each bud recalling to you a holy mystery; each ten bound together with my petition for a particular grace.

Or in Thanksgiving

Hail, Queen of the Most Holy Rosary, my Mother Mary, hail! At your feet I gratefully pray and offer to you a Crown of Roses — bright yellow roses to remind you of the ministry of your son — each bud recalling to you a holy mystery; each ten bound together with my petition for a particular grace.

Make the Sign of the Cross and pray the Creed, an Our Father, three Hail Marys, Glory Be, and Decade Prayer (see page 41).

I. The Baptism of Jesus in the Jordan River

O Courageous Mother Mary, meditating on the mystery of the baptism of Jesus in the Jordan River, when your son, as an example to all, insisted on being baptized by his cousin John and the sky opened and the Holy Spirit came down to him like a dove and a voice from heaven said, "You are my own dear Son in whom I am well pleased," I humbly pray:

Say an Our Father, ten Hail Marys, Glory Be, and Decade Prayer.

I bind these bright yellow roses with a petition for the virtue of Giving Good Example and humbly lay this bouquet at your feet.

II. The Wedding at Cana, Jesus' First Miracle

O Courageous Mother Mary, meditating on the mystery of the first miracle of Jesus at the wedding feast at Cana, when at your urging your son performed the first of his many miracles by helping a couple celebrate their marriage by changing water into wine of such quality that the chief steward upbraided the host by saying, "Usually people serve the best wine first and save the cheaper wine for last, but you have saved the choice wine for last," I humbly pray:

Say an Our Father, ten Hail Marys, Glory Be, and Decade Prayer.

I bind these bright yellow roses with a petition for the virtue of Responding the to Needs of Others and humbly lay this bouquet at your feet.

III. The Proclamation of the Kingdom of God

O courageous Mother Mary, meditating on the mystery of the proclamation of the Kingdom of God, when your son revealed that the reign of God has already begun "within us" and we are called to conversion and forgiveness, praying, "your Kingdom come, your will be done, on earth as it is in heaven," I humbly pray:

Say an Our Father, ten Hail Marys, Glory Be, and Decade Prayer.

I bind these bright yellow roses with a petition for the virtue of Working for Social Justice and humbly lay this bouquet at your feet.

IV. The Transfiguration

O courageous Mother Mary, meditating on the mystery of the Transfiguration, when your son revealed his glory to his three disciples, appearing on a mountain with Moses and Elijah, his face shining like the sun and a voice from heaven proclaiming, "This is my beloved Son...Listen to him," I humbly pray:

Say an Our Father, ten Hail Marys, Glory Be, and Decade Prayer.

I bind these bright yellow roses with a petition for the virtue of Listening to the Word of God and humbly lay this bouquet at your feet.

V. The Institution of the Eucharist

O courageous Mother Mary, meditating on the mystery of the institution of the Sacrament of the Eucharist, when on the day before he died your son celebrated the Passover with his disciples and took bread and gave it to them saying, "Take and eat; this is my body," and when dinner was finished he took a cup of wine and shared it with them saying, "Take and drink; this is my blood, which will be given up for you; do this in memory of me," I humbly pray:

Say an Our Father, ten Hail Marys, Glory Be, and Decade Prayer.

I bind these bright yellow roses with a petition for the virtue of Helping to Build the Faith Community and humbly lay this bouquet at your feet.

For the concluding prayers go to page 221.

THE SORROWFUL MYSTERIES

In petition

Hail, Queen of the Most Holy Rosary, my Mother Mary, Hail! At your feet I humbly pray and offer to you a Crown of Roses — blood-red roses to remind you of the passion of your divine Son, with whom you did so fully partake of its bitterness — each rose recalling to you a holy mystery; each ten bound together with my petition for a particular grace.

Or in Thanksgiving

Hail, Queen of the Most Holy Rosary, my Mother Mary, hail! At your feet I gratefully pray and offer to you a Crown of Roses — blood-red roses to remind you of the passion of your divine Son, with whom you did so fully partake of its bitterness — each rose recalling to you a holy mystery; each ten bound together with my petition for a particular grace.

Make the Sign of the Cross and pray the Creed, an Our Father, three Hail Marys, Glory Be, and Decade Prayer (see page 41).

I. The Agony in the Garden

O most sorrowful Mother Mary, meditating on the mystery of the agony of our Lord in the Garden, when, in the grotto of the Garden of Olives, Jesus saw the sins of the world unfold before him by Satan, who sought to dissuade him from the sacrifice he was about to make; when, his soul shrinking from the sight, and his precious blood flowing from every pore at the vision of the torture and death he was to undergo, your own sufferings, dear Mother, the future sufferings of his Church, and his own sufferings in the Blessed Sacraments, he cried in anguish, "Abba! Father! if it be possible, let this chalice pass from me!"; but, immediately resigning himself to his Father's will, he prayed, "Not as I will, but as you will," I humbly pray:

Say an Our Father, ten Hail Marys, Glory Be, and Decade Prayer.

I bind these blood-red roses with a petition for the virtue of Resignation to the Will of God and humbly lay this bouquet at your feet.

II. The Scourging at the Pillar

O most sorrowful Mother Mary, meditating on the mystery of the scourging of our Lord when, at Pilate's command, your divine Son, stripped of his garments and bound to a pillar, was lacerated from head to foot with cruel scourges and his flesh torn away until his mortified body could bear no more, I humbly pray:

Say an Our Father, ten Hail Marys, Glory Be, and Decade Prayer.

I bind these blood-red roses with a petition for the virtue of Forbearance and humbly lay this bouquet at your feet.

III. The Crowning with Thorns

O most sorrowful Mother Mary, meditating on the mystery of the crowning of our Lord with thorns, when, the soldiers, binding about his head a crown of sharp thorns, showered blows upon it, driving the thorns deeply into his head; then, in mock adoration, knelt before him, crying, "Hail, King of the Jews!" I humbly pray:

Say an Our Father, ten Hail Marys, Glory Be, and Decade Prayer.

I bind these blood-red roses with a petition for the virtue of Humility and humbly lay this bouquet at your feet.

IV. The Carrying of the Cross

O most sorrowful Mother Mary, meditating on the mystery of the carrying of the Cross, when, with the heavy wood of the cross upon his shoulders, your divine Son was dragged, weak and suffering, yet patient, through the streets, amidst the revilements of the people, to Calvary; falling often, but urged along by the cruel blows of his executioners, I humbly pray:

Say an Our Father, ten Hail Marys, Glory Be, and Decade Prayer.

I bind these blood-red roses with a petition for the virtue of Patience in Adversity and humbly lay this bouquet at your feet.

V. The Crucifixion

O most sorrowful Mother Mary, meditating on the mystery of the Crucifixion, when, having been stripped of the his garments, your divine Son was nailed to the cross, upon which he died after three hours of indescribable agony, during which time he begged from his Father, forgiveness for his enemies, I humbly pray:

Say an Our Father, ten Hail Marys, Glory Be, and Decade Prayer.

I bind these blood-red roses with a petition for the virtue of Love of Our Enemies and humbly lay this bouquet at your feet.

For the concluding prayers go to page 221.

THE GLORIOUS MYSTERIES

In petition

Hail, Queen of the Most Holy Rosary, my Mother Mary, Hail! At your feet I humbly pray and offer to you a Crown of Roses — full-blown royal purple roses, tinged with the red of passion, to remind you of your glories, fruits of the sufferings of your Son and you — each rose recalling to you a holy mystery; each ten bound together with my petition for a particular grace.

Or in Thanksgiving

Hail, Queen of the Most Holy Rosary, my Mother Mary, hail! At your feet I gratefully pray and offer to you a crown of roses — full-blown white roses, tinged with the red of passion, to remind you of your glories, fruits of the sufferings of your Son and you — each rose recalling to you a holy mystery; each ten bound together with my petition for a particular grace.

Make the Sign of the Cross and pray the Creed, an Our Father, three Hail Marys, Glory Be, and Decade Prayer (see page 41).

I. The Resurrection

O glorious Mother Mary, meditating on the mystery of the Resurrection of our Lord from the dead, when, on the morning of the third day after his death and burial, he arose from the dead and appeared to you, dear Mother, and filled your heart with unspeakable joy; then appeared to the holy women, and to his disciples, who adored him as their risen God, I humbly pray:

Say an Our Father, ten Hail Marys, Glory Be, and Decade Prayer.

I bind these full-blown roses with a petition for the virtue of Faith and humbly lay this bouquet at your feet.

II. The Ascension

O glorious Mother Mary, meditating on the mystery of the Ascension, when your divine Son, after forty days on earth, went to Mount Olivet accompanied by his disciples and you, where all adored him for the last time, after which he promised to remain with them until the end of the world; then, extending his pierced hands over all in a last blessing, he ascended before their eyes into heaven, I humbly pray:

Say an Our Father, ten Hail Marys, Glory Be, and Decade Prayer.

I bind these full-blown roses with a petition for the virtue of Hope and humbly lay this bouquet at your feet.

III. The Descent of the Holy Spirit

O glorious Mother Mary, meditating on the mystery of the descent of the Holy Spirit, when, the apostles being assembled with you in a house and Jerusalem, the Holy Spirit descended upon them in the form of fiery tongues, inflaming the hearts of the apostles with the fire of divine love, teaching them all truths, giving to them the gift of tongues, and, filling you with the plenitude of his grace, inspired you to pray for the apostles and the first Christians, I humbly pray:

Say an Our Father, ten Hail Marys, Glory Be, and Decade Prayer.

I bind these full-blown roses with a petition for the virtue of Charity and humbly lay this bouquet at your feet

IV. The Assumption of Our Blessed Mother into Heaven

O glorious Mother Mary, meditating on the mystery of your Assumption into Heaven, when, consumed with the desire to be united with your divine Son in heaven, your soul departed from your body and united itself to him, who, out of the excessive love he bore for you, his Mother, whose virginal body was his first tabernacle, took that body into heaven and there, amidst the acclaims of the angels and saints, reinfused into it your soul, I humbly pray:

Say an Our Father, ten Hail Marys, Glory Be, and Decade Prayer.

I bind these full-blown roses with a petition for the virtue of Union with Christ and humbly lay this bouquet at your feet.

V. The Coronation of Our Blessed Mother

O glorious Mother Mary, meditating on the mystery of your Coronation in Heaven, when, upon being taken up to heaven after your death, you were triply crowned as the august Queen of Heaven by God the Father as his beloved Daughter, by God the Son as his dearest Mother, and by God the Holy Spirit as his chosen Spouse; the most perfect adorer of the Blessed Trinity, leading our cause as our most powerful and merciful Mother, through you, I humbly pray:

Say an Our Father, ten Hail Marys, Glory Be, and Decade Prayer.

I bind these full-blown roses with a petition for the virtue of Union with you and humbly lay this bouquet at your feet.

Pray the concluding prayers on page 221.

The Concluding Prayers for all the Mysteries

Spiritual Communion

My Jesus, really present in the most holy Sacrament of the Altar, since I cannot now receive you under the sacramental veil, I beseech you, with a heart full of love and longing, to come spiritually into my soul through the immaculate heart of your most holy Mother, and abide with me forever: you in me, and I in you, in time and in eternity, in Mary.

In petition

Sweet Mother Mary, I offer you this Spiritual Communion to bind my bouquets in a wreath to place upon your brow.

O my Mother! Look with favor upon my gift, and your love obtained for me *[specified requests]*.

Or in thanksgiving

Sweet Mother Mary, I offer you this Spiritual Communion to bind my bouquets in a wreath to place upon your brow in thanksgiving for *[specified requests]* that you in your love have obtained for me.

Hail, Holy Queen
See page 20.

Prayer to Saint Michael
See page 21.

The Litany of the Blessed Virgin Mary
See pages 176–179.

NOVENA RECORD

Use these charts to record your daily recitation of the Rosary.

In petition

Day 1	Day 2	Day 3	Day 4	Day 5	Day 6	Day 7	Day 8	Day 9
Day 10	Day 11	Day 12	Day 13	Day 14	Day 15	Day 16	Day 17	Day 18
Day 19	Day 20	Day 21	Day 22	Day 23	Day 24	Day 25	Day 26	Day 27

In thanksgiving

Day 1	Day 2	Day 3	Day 4	Day 5	Day 6	Day 7	Day 8	Day 9
Day 10	Day 11	Day 12	Day 13	Day 14	Day 15	Day 16	Day 17	Day 18
Day 19	Day 20	Day 21	Day 22	Day 23	Day 24	Day 25	Day 26	Day 27

APPENDIX A

WORKS OF MERCY AND OTHER GUIDELINES

THE SEVEN CORPORAL WORKS OF MERCY

Feed the hungry.
Give drink to the thirsty.
Clothe the naked.
Shelter the homeless.
Visit the sick.
Visit the imprisoned.
Bury the dead.

THE SEVEN SPIRITUAL WORKS OF MERCY

Instruct the ignorant.
Counsel the doubtful.
Admonish sinners.
Bear wrongs patiently.
Forgive offenses willingly.
Comfort the afflicted.
Pray for the living and the dead.

THE TWELVE FRUITS OF THE SPIRIT

Charity • Generous actions or donations to aid the poor, ill, or helpless; leniency in judging others; forbearance.

Joy • The emotion of great delight or happiness caused by something exceptionally good or satisfying.

Peace • Freedom of the mind from annoyance, distraction, anxiety, or obsession.

Patience • The bearing of provocation, annoyance, misfortune, or pain without complaint, loss of temper, or irritation.

Kindness • Having compassion, sympathy; being thoughtful.

Goodness • Moral excellence; virtue.

Long-suffering • Extraordinary patience under provocation or trial; patient endurance of hardship, injuries, or offense; forbearance.

Gentleness • Amiably gentle or temperate in feeling or behavior toward others.

Faithfulness • Trusting in God's promises as made through Christ and the Scriptures by which humans are justified or saved.

Modesty • Freedom from vanity, boastfulness; simplicity; moderation.

Self-control • Self-restraint or abstinence; temperance; moderation.

Chastity • The state or quality of being pure, free from obscene thoughts or actions; sexual abstinence, especially before marriage.

SUPERNATURAL VIRTUES

Faith
Hope
Charity

CARDINAL VIRTUES

Prudence
Justice
Temperance

THE SEVEN CAPITAL VIRTUES

Humility
Liberality
Brotherly love
Meekness
Chastity
Temperance
Diligence

PRECEPTS OF THE CHURCH

1. You shall attend Mass on Sundays and the holy days of obligation and rest from servile labor.

2. You shall confess your sins at least once a year.

3. You shall receive the sacrament of the Eucharist at least during the Easter season.

4. You shall observe the days of abstinence and fasting established by the Church.

    Every person fourteen years of age or older must abstain from meat (and items made with meat) on Ash Wednesday, Good Friday, and all the Fridays of Lent.

    Every person between the age of eighteen and sixty must fast on Ash Wednesday and Good Friday.

    Every person fourteen years of age or older must abstain from meat (and items made with meat) on all other Fridays of the year, unless he or she substitutes some other form of penance for abstinence.

5. You shall help to provide for the needs of the Church.

The two listed below are not official precepts, but are mentioned elsewhere in the *Catechism of the Catholic Church*.

6. You shall observe the marriage laws of the Church.

7. You are to join in the missionary spirit and apostolate of the Church.

THE SEVEN CARDINAL SINS

The cardinal sins are pride, avarice (greed), envy, wrath, lust, gluttony, sloth.

We conquer *pride* by the practice of *humility*.

We conquer *greed* by the practice of *liberality*.

We conquer *envy* through the practice of *brotherly love*.

We conquer *wrath* by the practice of *meekness*.

We conquer *lust* through the practice of *chastity*.

We conquer *gluttony* by the consistent practice of *temperance* and by reflecting on Jesus' words:

> "Do not work for the food that perishes,
> but for the food that endures for eternal life." (John 6:27).

We conquer *sloth* by the practice of *diligence*.

APPENDIX B
PRAYER FOR THE DEAD

A PRAYER FOR THE DEAD

O gentlest heart of Jesus, ever present in the Blessed Sacrament, ever consumed with burning love for the poor captive souls in Purgatory, have mercy on the souls of your servants: *[List the names of the dead on this and following pages and mention them here].*

Be not severe in your judgment but let some drops of your Precious Blood fall upon the devouring flames, and do you, O merciful Savior send your angels to conduct your servants to a place of refreshment, light, and peace. Amen.

See also page 170.

Name	Date of Death

Name   **Date of Death**

Name   Date of Death

Name	Date of Death

Name   Date of Death

Name	Date of Death

NOTES

NOTES

Use these pages to record reflections, intentions, additional prayers, novenas, and litanies.

NOTES

NOTES

NOTES

NOTES

NOTES

INDEX

Act of Charity 18
Act of Consecration to the Holy Spirit 196
Act of Contrition 17, 71
Act of Faith 17
Act of Hope 18
Act of Reparation 105
Act of Reparation to the Sacred Heart of Jesus 144
Adoration of the Blessed Sacrament 109
Angelus 19
Apostles' Creed 16

Brown Scapular 93

Canticle of Mary 117
Chaplet, Divine Mercy 111
Christmas 182
Church, Precepts of the 228
Confession 59
Confiteor 18

Daily Meditation, Subjects for 38
Daily Prayers
   Afternoon 35
   Bedtime 37
   Dawn 31
   Evening 36
   Midday 34
   Morning 32
Dead, Prayer for, and Record 233
Decade Prayer 42
Devotions
   Brown Scapular 93
   Divine Mercy 111
   First Five Saturdays 94

Devotions, continued
   First Fridays 103
   Miraculous Medal 110
   Our Lady of Fatima 94
   Sacred Heart of Jesus 102
   Seven Sorrows of Mary 99
   Divine Mercy 35, 111
   Divine Mercy Chaplet 111

Exaltation of the Holy Cross 158
Examination of Conscience, Samples of 59
   Simple 60
   Thorough 61

Fatima Prayers 97
Feast Days
   All Saints 168
   All Souls 170
   Annunciation of the Lord 138
   Archangels 162
   Ascension 195
   Assumption of the Blessed Virgin Mary 156
   Chair of Saint Peter 134
   Christmas 182
   Corpus Christi 201
   Dedication of the Lateran Basilica 171
   Divine Mercy 113, 187
   Easter 186
   Exaltation of the Holy Cross 158
   Immaculate Conception of the Blessed Virgin Mary 175
   Most Holy Name of Mary 158
   Nativity of Saint John the Baptist 147
   Nativity of the Blessed Virgin Mary 158
   Nativity of the Lord (Christmas) 182

Feast Days, continued
    Our Lady of Guadalupe 179
    Our Lady of Lourdes 127
    Passion of John the Baptist 157
    Pentecost 196
    Presentation of the Blessed Virgin Mary 172
    Presentation of the Lord 127
    Queenship of the Blessed Virgin Mary 157
    Sacred Heart 144
    Solemnity of Mary, Mother of God 117, 184
    The Holy Innocents 183
    Transfiguration of the Lord 156
    Trinity Sunday 200
    Visitation of the Blessed Virgin Mary 143
First Friday Devotions 103

Glorious Mysteries 49, 217
Grace After Meals 28
Grace Before Meals 26

Hail, Holy Queen 20
Hail Mary 16
Hour of Mercy 35, 112

Jesus Prayer 18
Joyful Mysteries 43, 213

Litanies
    Blessed Virgin Mary 176
    Our Lady of Lourdes 132
    Our Lady of Prompt Succor 119
    Sacred Heart 107
    Saints 168
Luminous Mysteries 45, 209

Magnificat 117
Mary, Help of Christians 143
Mass 53
   Eucharistic Fast 53
   Prayer After Communion 56
   Prayer Before Communion 55
   Prayers Before Mass 54
   Prayers During 54
Medal of the Immaculate Conception 110
Memorare 23
Mercy, Works of 225
Miraculous Medal 110
Most Holy Name of Mary 158

Name of Jesus 24
Novena Record, Rosary 222
Novenas
   Annunciation of the Lord 138
   Ascension 195
   Chaplets to the Divine Mercy 113
   Christmas 182
   Divine Mercy 187
   Easter 186
   Grace of Saint Francis Xavier 136
   Immaculate Conception of the Blessed Virgin Mary 175
   John Vianney 155
   Nativity of the Lord (Christmas) 182
   Our Lady of Fatima 142
   Our Lady of Guadalupe 179
   Our Lady of Lourdes 127
   Our Lady of Mount Carmel 150
   Our Lady of Prompt Succor 118
   Our Lady of Sorrows 158

Novenas, continued
>   Our Lady of the Rosary 165
>   Our Mother of Perpetual Help 147
>   Pentecost 196
>   Record for Rosary Novena 222
>   Rosary Novena to Our Lady 203
>   Sacred Heart of Jesus 146, 201
>   Saint Anne 153
>   Saint Anthony 201
>   Saint Joseph 137
>   Saint Philomena 155
>   Saint Thérèse of the Child Jesus 164

Our Father 15
Our Lady of Fatima 94, 142
Our Lady of Guadalupe 179
Our Lady of Mount Carmel 150
Our Lady of Prompt Succor 118
Our Lady of Sorrows 158
Our Lady of Tepeyac 25
Our Lady of the Rosary 165
Our Mother of Perpetual Help 147

Prayers 15
>   Act of Charity 18
>   Act of Consecration to the Holy Spirit 196
>   Act of Contrition 17, 18
>   Act of Faith 17
>   Act of Hope 18
>   Act of Reparation 105
>   Act of Reparation to the Sacred Heart of Jesus 144
>   Angelus 19
>   Apostles' Creed 16
>   Bernadette, Saint 140

252 • IN THIS TIME OF MERCY

Prayers, continued
  Communion, After 56
  Communion, Before 55
  Confiteor 18
  Crucifix, Before a 22
  Dead, For the 170
  Decade Prayer 42
  Divine Mercy Chaplet 111
  Fatima 97
  Francis of Assisi 164
  Glory Be 16
  Grace After Meals 28
  Grace Before Meals 26
  Hail, Holy Queen 20
  Hail Mary 16
  Immaculate Heart of Mary 32
  Jesus, Name of 24
  Jesus Prayer 18
  Joseph, Saint 22
  Kateri Tekakwitha 149
  Legal Protection of Unborn Children, For the 123
  Lent and Passiontide, Fridays of 186
  Mass, Before 54
  Mass, During 54
  Memorare 23
  Michael, Saint 21
  Miraculous Trust 25
  Our Father 15
  Precious Blood Offering 23
  Queen of Heaven 20
  Regina Caeli 20
  Rosary 41
  Sacred Heart of Jesus, Consecration to the 104

Prayers, continued
    Sacred Heart of Jesus, Daily Offering to the 32
    Sacred Heart, To the 56
    Serenity 24
    Seven Gifts of the Holy Spirit, For the 197
    Sign of the Cross 15
    Te Deum 184
    Thanks 23
    Thomas Aquinas, Saint 55
    Trinity, In Praise of the 200
Precepts of the Church 228
Precious Blood Offering 23

Reconciliation, Sacrament of 59
    Examination of Conscience, Simple 60
    Examination of Conscience, Thorough 61
    Prayers During 70
Rosary 41, 165
    Glorious Mysteries 49
    Joyful Mysteries 43
    Luminous Mysteries 45
    Novena to Our Lady 203
        Concluding Prayers for All Mysteries 221
        Glorious Mysteries 217
        Joyful Mysteries 205
        Luminous Mysteries 209
        Novena Record 222
        Sorrowful Mysteries 213
    Sorrowful Mysteries 47

Sacred Heart of Jesus 102, 144
Saints
    Agatha of Sicily 127
    Agnes of Rome 123

Saints, continued
  Aloysius Gonzaga 147
  Alphonsus Liguori 99, 155
  Ambrose of Milan 175
  André Bessette 118
  Andrew 172
  Andrew Dũng-Lạc of Vietnam 172
  Andrew Kim Tae-gŏn of Korea 162
  Anne 153
  Anthony of Padua 147, 201
  Athanasius 142
  Augustine of Hippo 157
  Barnabas 147
  Bartholomew 157
  Basil the Great 118
  Benedict 149
  Bernadette of Lourdes 127, 140
  Bernard 157
  Blaise 127
  Bonaventure 150
  Bridget of Sweden 99
  Camillus de Lellis 152
  Catherine Labouré 110
  Catherine of Siena 141
  Cecilia 172
  Charles Borromeo 171
  Clare 156
  Cornelius 162
  Cyprian 162
  Damien de Veuster of Moloka'i 142
  Dominic 156
  Elizabeth Ann Seton 118
  Elizabeth of Hungary 99, 172

Saints, continued
  Elizabeth of Portugal 149
  Frances Xavier Cabrini 172
  Francis of Assisi 164
  Francis Xavier 174
  Francis Xavier Seelos (Blessed) 165
  Gabriel 162
  Gregory Nazianzen 118
  Gregory the Great 158
  Ignatius of Antioch 166
  Isaac Jogues 166
  Isidore 142
  James 152
  Jerome 163
  Joachim and Anne 153
  John 183
  John Baptist de La Salle 140
  John Chrysostom 158
  John de Brébeuf 166
  John Neumann 118
  John Paul II 43, 45, 47, 49, 166
  John Vianney 155
  John XXIII 166
  Josaphat 172
  Joseph 22, 137
  Juan Diego of Mexico 179
  Jude 166
  Junípero Serra 149
  Justin Martyr 144
  Kateri Tekakwitha 149
  Katharine Drexel 136
  Lawrence 156
  Leo the Great 171

Saints, continued
  Lucy of Syracuse 182
  Luke 166
  Margaret Mary Alacoque 103
  Maria Faustina Kowalska 7, 111
  Marianne Cope of Moloka'i 126
  Marie Durocher (Blessed) 165
  Mark 141
  Martha 154
  Martin of Tours 171
  Mary Magdalene 152
  Matthew 162
  Matthias 142
  Michael 21, 162
  Miguel Agustin Pro (Blessed) 172
  North American Martyrs 166
  Paul Chŭng Ha-Sang of Korea 162
  Paul Miki of Japan 127
  Paul of the Cross 166
  Paul the Apostle 126
  Peter and Paul 148
  Peter Claver 158
  Philip Neri 143
  Philomena 155
  Pius of Pietrelcina 162
  Pius X 53
  Raphael 162
  Rose Philippine Duchesne 172
  Simon 166
  Simon Stock 93
  Stanislaus 140
  Stephen 183
  Teresa of Jesus (Avila) 7, 166

Saints, continued
    Thérèse of the Child Jesus 164
    Thomas Aquinas 126
    Timothy 126
    Titus 126
    Vincent de Paul 162
    Vincent of Saragossa 126
Serenity Prayer 24
Seven Sorrows of Mary 99
Sign of the Cross 15
Sins
    Accessory to Another's Sin 60
    Mortal 59
    Seven Cardinal 229
Sorrowful Mysteries 47, 213
Spirit
    Twelve Fruits of 226
Stations of the Cross 75
    Preparatory Prayer 75

Te Deum 184

Virtues
    Cardinal 227
    Seven Capital 227
    Supernatural 227

Works of Mercy
    Seven Corporal 225
    Seven Spiritual 225

PRAYER RESOURCES FROM ACTA PUBLICATIONS

Rosary Novenas to Our Lady
(Including the Mysteries of Light)
Charles B. Lacy; revised by Gregory F.A. Pierce
48 pages, paperback in standard size, large print, and Spanish
Original edition also available

The Rosary Prayer-by-Prayer
Mary K. Doyle
212 pages, paperback

The Forgiveness Book: A Catholic Approach
Alice Camille and Paul Boudreau
112 pages, paperback

Angel Devotion Prayerbook
compiled by Luis Valverde
50 pages, paperback

CDs
The Rosary (including the Mysteries of Light)
El Rosario (con los Misterios Luminosos)
Lenten Devotions
The Stations of the Cross and Seven Last Words
Scriptural Meditations for the Divine Mercy Chaplet
A Catholic Prayer Companion
Treasury of Catholic Devotions

DVD
The Rosary and Stations of the Cross

Available from Booksellers or ACTA Publications
800-397-2282 • www.actapublications.com